THE
SEVENTH
SUNRISE

A TIME TO HEAR GOD'S WHISPER

Susie —

MAY YOU ALWAYS SHINE
IN HIS LOVING LIGHT !

Larry Gordon

LARRY GORDON

ISBN 978-1-63844-553-1 (paperback)
ISBN 979-8-88685-915-7 (hardcover)
ISBN 978-1-63844-554-8 (digital)

Christian Faith Publishing
832 Park Avenue
Meadville, PA 16335
www.christianfaithpublishing.com

Printed in the United States of America

CONTENTS

PREFACE

This year marks the seventh year of my retirement. Some say that the number seven is lucky, especially if triple sevens come up on your slot machine in Las Vegas. However, the number seven can also mean transformation.

Some scientists say that the earth transforms its energy every seven thousand years. Human beings change their cellular levels, and the skeletal bone structure renews itself every seven years.

The Bible mentions the number seven more than seven hundred times. Seven symbolizes completeness and perfection. Moses brought down seven plagues to free the Israelites from Pharaoh. God created the world in six days and rested on the seventh.

Jesus gave us the Lord's Prayer, which consists of seven petitions. Our Lord spoke his last seven words while he was on the cross, and the world changed forever!

One thing that has changed for me in my retirement is that I no longer need clocks or alarms. I now wake up to the sunrise; whether it is 5:30 a.m. in June or 7:15 a.m. in November, I usually wake up a few minutes before dawn.

Whether I am gazing out from my bedroom window, perched on a nearby mountainside, or sitting in my camp chair on the prairie, my appreciation of sunrises grows with each day.

The Seventh Sunrise is a collection of thoughts and reflections on life's momentous events with all its elations and melancholy.

It also includes observations on the sometimes-unnoticed little blessings that God may have sprinkled in on each of those days of creation.

I have just hiked up on Granite Mountain to a spot where my effort is about to be rewarded.

For the next seven glorious minutes, as the sunlight hits our atmosphere, God will paint the sky with an incredible array of color.

It seems as though no two sunrises are the same. Each one has its canvas, its portrait to share, and its celebration of a new day.

And with each sunrise begins another story, a time for joy, a time for sorrow but, most of all, a time to care!

It's going to be a beautiful day!

Day One

First is this, God created the heavens and earth—all you see, all you don't see. Earth was a soup of nothingness, a bottomless emptiness, an inky blackness. God's spirit brooded like a bird above the watery abyss.

God spoke, "Light!" And light appeared. God saw that light was good and separated light from dark. God named the light Day; he named the dark Night. It was evening, it was morning—Day One.

I LOVE SUNRISES

In Him was life, and that life was the light of
all mankind. The light shines in the darkness,
and the darkness did not overcome it!

—John 1:4–5 NRSV

When one becomes threescore and fifteen, the truth is that
he must realize he has seen way more sunsets than he will
ever see sunrises. And that makes each new dawning in his
life all the more beautiful.

For every sunrise marks the beginning of a new daily
performance in his life. Now the stage is set, the curtain rises,
and the lights are focused on the next day in his life.

Did you know, at twenty-seven weeks from conception,
just before the third trimester, the fetus can open its eyes
from inside the womb and see the light coming in from the
outside?

In the animal kingdom, blindness at birth serves to pre-
serve the young who are dependent on their parents. This
premise makes a lot of sense. If they could see, they might
wander off to be eaten by predators.

However, the very first sense a human has is not sight
but the sense of touch. Our Lord gave us the ability to feel
the presence of another human being before anything else—
how amazing!

I think the fox was so right when he counseled the little prince, "It's only with the heart that one can see clearly. What's essential is invisible to the eye!"

It is mid-August as I sit in my chair on the Arizona chaparral. Sunrise has come and gone. The cirrus swirls, have turned from gray to saffron, and then disappeared into a sea of azure. Now the sky is streaked with the pale contrails of east and westbound aircraft. I wonder who will greet their cargo when they land?

Every afternoon for the next few weeks, the monsoons make their pilgrimage—first with claps of thunder, then followed by a torrent of water, filling every parched desert nook and cranny, only to be followed by silent rainbows.

Perhaps God gave us storms in our lives to nudge us into becoming closer with our brothers and sisters. So often we lose track of those who suffer in silence.

Why is it that those who roam through our land, our neighborhood, find that our streets are narrow, and our walls are tall, and our minds are closed?

What welcome mat are they seeking? Could it be they long to be with someone who truly listens?

Why is it that the broken find a way to shine on others while some of those on the straight and narrow never see the light of day?

Are we on a mission, on a journey, or only on a casual stroll? Could it be that we have found a way to outpace our daily parade?

Some walk in cadence; others run with a passion; and a few sit in a lotus position in the middle of life's highway, oblivious to the oncoming traffic. Others pass by, never glancing in their rearview mirror to notice that wounded solitary figure getting smaller and smaller until it fades out of sight.

I hurried from one appointment to another during my career, carried by four wheels, or buckled in at thirty-five thousand feet. Funny thing about jet aircraft, they have no rearview mirrors!

When you ache with need and are stripped down, stripped naked, lost in that desert highway's mirage, only then are you ready to hear God's whisper!

It is four o'clock now, and I can hear the gentle rhythm of rain droplets falling from the eaves of my dwelling.

I love sunrises!

> The stars, that nature hung in heaven, and filled their lamps with ever-lasting oil, give due light to the misled and lonely traveler.
>
> —John Milton

'TIS A PUZZLEMENT

Have patience, God isn't finished yet.

—Philippians 1:6

The King of Siam mused while the world changed so much since he was a boy. Now he is a man, and all he can declare is "'tis a puzzlement!"

Don't we all have questions that seem to go unanswered in life? Sometimes these are crazy questions that even provoke our conscience: If someone calls an ambulance to save a life, and that ambulance mortally hits someone on the way to the caller, should that ambulance stop to save the person who got hit?

Our priorities always seem to get sidetracked by others in need as we make our way through life's labyrinth.

When I was growing up in Los Angeles, life seemed to be happy and uncomplicated. The sounds of automobiles and buses making their way down the streets of my neighborhood served as familiar background music while we played on our school grounds.

Of course the sounds of sirens and helicopters always got our attention. I remember my older sister making the sign of the cross to the wail of an ambulance speeding by. No wonder she became a nurse.

The seeds of my faith sprouted just a few days after I turned seven in the Immaculate Heart of Mary Catholic Church in Hollywood, California, when I was trained by a nun to receive my first communion.

When I arrived at her class, I remember Sister Fran coming up to me, crouching down, playfully pinching my cheeks, pointing at me, raising her arms, and declaring, "*You are a precious child of God!*"

As she taught the class, I became convinced that she knew everything there was to know about church and God.

So I asked her, "Where does God live?"

"Where do you think he lives?" said she.

So I asked her, "Could he be living in that shiny box up there on the altar?"

"Oh, yes!" said she as she attended to my other classmates.

I accepted her answer because whenever the priest passed by the box, he bowed and treated it with a lot of honor and respect. Besides, the box had a roof, four walls, a sliding door, and what looked like a solid gold frame!

I then concluded that God didn't have any hands because the door to the box had no knob! The priest just used his thumb to open and close God's house.

When our class sat together during high mass, I whispered to Sister Fran seated behind me, "Does God come and go with that sweet smelling smoke?"

This time I felt a firm tapping on my shoulder as she put her other hand to her lips and went, "Shush!"

I was too afraid to ask the father if his singing coaxed God out of his dwelling. I smelled the aroma and heard the chimes but saw no God!

After that, my questions about God's whereabouts were asked by me to only me. *Does he live in the clouds, on a mountaintop, behind the stars?*

On Saturdays, I would go to the movies with my older sister and her friends. I saw the movie *The Robe* and later *The Ten Commandments.* Now the possible answers to my questions came with sound and Technicolor!

Sister Fran told me that I had to confess and say to the father all of my sins to receive communion.

"All?" said I.

"All!" said she.

She taught me to recite the confessional prayer as if it were a greeting to the strange shadow behind the veiled curtain.

"Bless me, father, for I have sinned."

After naming what I thought were all my sins, the veiled figure gave me an assignment.

"Go out and say twelve Hail Marys and six Our Fathers, my son."

As I exited the booth, my young mind kept asking, "All?

"All!"

I decided to leave the Roman Catholic Church and became a Lutheran while I was in college. After studying the word, it started to speak to me. Old Testament scripture blended with New Testament gospel so that the pieces to God's story fit.

Then I read Psalm 91 NIV, "Whoever dwells in the shelter of the Most High will rest in the shadow of the Almighty. I will say to the Lord, He is my refuge and my fortress." And there in the midst of that dorm room appeared the answer to my childhood question. He not only lives in the box and the book but in me!

I finally found my Lord and Savior!

I think my faith became more defined four decades ago when my pastor asked if I would teach a confirmation class. At first I avoided eye contact. Then I hesitantly looked at him and asked, "But how will I know if the kids will be interested in what I have to say?"

He thought for a second, then with his eyes focused above the rim of his glasses, he said in an exaggerated tone, "Oh, you'll know. Just be yourself, and tell God's story as best you can!"

As that first class began, I started telling God's story, and a question immediately came up. This time the question from student to teacher wasn't "Where does God live?" but "What is faith anyway?" So I told them the story of the tightrope walker and his wheelbarrow.

"Think of it this way," said I, "Close your eyes, and imagine you are one hundred stories up on the roof of a magnificent skyscraper. As you walk over to the edge, you see there is a tightrope strung from your building to another. As the wind is howling, the tightrope walker gets on the rope and slowly pushes his wheelbarrow to the other side. You are amazed. You call out to the tightrope walker, 'Come back, I need you to return. Only this time, could you load your wheelbarrow with two hundred pounds of rocks in it?' The tightrope walker does as you ask and returns with ease."

"Now the tightrope walker has a challenge for you. He asks you to get inside the wheelbarrow, and he will push you to the other side. Would you do it? After all, you know he is capable of it. He just proved it to you, not once but twice."

After asking this question to more than eight hundred confirmation students over the next forty years, I have had only a handful say they would have eagerly taken the dare. But even these aspiring daredevils had to admit that they had just a twinge of hesitation before climbing in that wheelbarrow. They, just like everyone else, were afraid that the tight-rope walker just might slip. And in his falling, so would you. But with you in the barrow and God pushing from behind, He will always get you to the other side—no worries! You see, belief and trust have to go hand in hand for it to be true faith. Just as Proverbs 3:5–6 NIV declares, "Trust in the Lord with all your heart, and lean not on your own understanding, in all your ways submit to him, and he will make your paths straight!"

Sometimes the most difficult questions that test our faith come to us when we are helpless, hopeless, and hurting. When you can't see the path in front of you, and the horizon seems to melt away as the sun goes down.

As I watch a new sunrise appear over this desert, the words of Sister Fran continue to echo in my mind, reminding me that each of us is a "precious child of God!"

As to that next sunrise on the horizon, well…

"'Tis a puzzlement!"

Truly I tell you, if you have faith as small as a mustard seed, you can say to this mountain, "Move from here to there," and it will move. Nothing will be impossible to you.

—Matthew 17:20 NIV

THE KING'S MEADOW

Consider the lilies how they grow: they neither
toil nor spin; yet I tell you, even Solomon, in all
his glory, was not clothed like one of these.

—Luke 12:27 NRSV

Blessings came down from heaven a few months ago when
my sixth great-grandchild was born. Her name is Kinsley.
The name comes from an English origin and means "the
king's meadow."

I am blessed, you see. For now I have held all of my
great-grandchildren in my arms. My wife was able to have
hugged and kissed our very first great-grandchild before she
passed away.

People keep advising me, "You should travel and see the
world while you're in your golden years." The only trips I've
taken lately have been visiting friends and family scattered
from Florida to Alaska.

Now I realize that I will probably be gone well before
my great-grandchildren are hopefully living their lives to the
fullest and making their way on God's green earth.

But in a way, aren't we all romping through the king's
meadow? If you're lucky enough, maybe you dance through
it!

Some sit and picnic in it while admiring the beauty; others play in it while adding to the joy in their lives. And still others trample on it, ignoring the one commandment the king has decreed, "You must take care of this place; otherwise you will lose it forever!"

When I was a young man, carefree, and in college, roaming through the king's meadow, my world changed forever. As I look back on my life with all its blessings and regrets, I miss her just a little more today than yesterday.

It was on a Sunday afternoon, in the spring, when the pastel colors of the tree blossoms swayed against a blue sky. It was the day I met Wendy.

Within an hour of our introduction, we were dancing to the tune of the Lettermen's song "When I Fall in Love." Throughout the years, we recalled that moment. And in our reminiscing, we would relive it as we danced in our living room without music as we hummed our song's melody.

But I think it was in the fall when the cold crisp New England air hit our faces, driven by our ice skates' motion, did our love begin to gel.

Could it be that the pull of passion can cause one to push away abruptly and slap the other's cheek? Only ten days from our introduction did she leave me for a young sailor named Mark.

Wendy was not ready for a lasting relationship, abandoned by her father at the age of ten and another boy at sixteen who she thought she loved after giving up his child for adoption.

I was devastated the night she left me. And while I went out with others, I was in a fog. Then four months later, she called and asked me if we could resume the dance, and the dancing never ceased!

A year and a half later, we ran off and eloped in Idaho. She was only eighteen, and I had just turned twenty. There was a justice of the peace and a Paiute Native American woman to serve as witness. Wendy looked beautiful in her blue and white tweed dress as I stood next to her in my mohair sport coat. The Paiute lady smiled as we exchanged vows, and blessed us at the end. She quoted part of an old Apache proverb, "May your days be good and long upon the earth."

Half a century later, after raising our children in California and living our empty nest years in New England, we found our golden years home in the Arizona desert. And she asked me, "Where are all the trees?"

It was 3:00 a.m. as I got up from Wendy's hospital room recliner. She seemed to be comfortably asleep in her ICU bed. I remember thinking that the whole hospital seemed empty, save my wife and I. All I could hear was the drone of various life-sustaining machines and an occasional chime.

As I ventured out of her ICU unit, I passed by one hospital room after another, wondering, *Whose life is in peril tonight?* The hallway lights were dimmed for those who sleep.

I wandered down the hallways of St. Joseph's in my zombie-like trance, staring at the shuffle of my feet. Every few minutes, I would look up to see yet another inspirational biblical quote lasered on an adorned religious painting.

Most of them were comforting words from Jesus. One read the words of John 14:2–3 NIV:

> My father's house has many rooms; if that were not so, would I have told you that I am going there to prepare a place for you? And if I go and prepare a place for you, I will come back and take you to

be with me that you also may be where I
am. You know the way to the place where
I am going.

My roving brought me to the entrance to the hospital
chapel. Before entering the vacant sanctuary, I glanced at the
guest book mounted on a waist-high pedestal. It contained
a collection of prayer requests and petitions. Each seemed to
have one common plea: "Please Lord, guide the hands of our
surgeon and bring my loved one through safely."

My prayer stayed within me as I sat alone in the chapel
pew. It was only an unanswered question waiting for a sign.
Her brain surgery was successful and gave us a few more
weeks to be together.

As she lay in her hospice bed with our dance but a gentle sway, I came to her with a picture of where we would rest
under the shade of a magnificent juniper tree overlooking the
high desert mountains.

I saw a smile, felt a gentle squeeze on my hand, and
shared one last kiss.

Now the dance can be seen on our eleven grandchildren
and seven great-grandchildren's faces. It is satisfying to know
that their dances in the king's meadow started on a spring day
so many years ago.

Yes, it was on a Sunday afternoon when I met my
Wendy!

Love bears all things, believes all things,
hopes all things, endures all things.

—1 Corinthians 13:7 NRSV

ME AND GOD ARE WATCHING SCOTTY GROW

The soul would have no rainbow if the eyes had no tears.

—Native American Proverb

As I sit on my bedroom porch, the wind chimes, catalyze to transport me back into a happier time to a place called Angel's Flight in the Sierra Nevada Mountains.

My nine-year-old son, Scotty, and I were traversing a trail where the switchbacks etch into Carson Peak's granite face. The whistle of the wind intensified our adventure as we looked down an eighteen-hundred-foot drop.

Our destination was a small high-country body of water called Thousand Island Lake.

We had been hiking the trail for about two hours when we stopped to rest. We leaned against the granite wall of the mountain to avoid taking our backpacks off. I reached into Scotty's pack to find two sandwiches consisting of peanut butter and jelly. The remnants of the squished bread dough caused our sandwiches to look more like a ball than a square.

As we were standing up, Scotty asked, "How come seagulls fly way up to these mountains? Why aren't they flying over the sea?"

"Guess they prefer rainbows over mackerel," I answered.

"Wish I was a seagull. It would be so much easier to get to the lake," he said. "How much longer do we have to get there, Dad?" That was at least the eleventh time he asked me.

I answer in the voice of Maxwell Smart, "Would you beeleeeve, three more hours?"

"Uh uh," he grunted.

"Sorry about that, chief," I replied. "Let's keep moving!"

So here we were, camped near the shore of this beautiful pristine lake, ten thousand feet above sea level.

The air was crisp, and the panorama was stunning. Mount Ritter and Banner Peak glistened in the distance revealing a patchwork of snow against a deep cerulean sky. The only sound in the moment was that of water running over rocks from melting ice.

After a dinner consisting of dehydrated au gratin potatoes, spinach, and trout, we crawled into our sleeping bags. I woke up a few hours later and reached over to Scotty's sleeping bag—and no Scotty!

And just as I started to panic and yell out, I heard Scotty shouting from the outside of the tent.

"Dad, dad, come out here quick!"

Well I bolted out of the tent and saw Scotty standing by the shore. He pointed out on the lake and exclaimed, "It's just like Fantasy Island!"

You see, our campsite was next to this little stream that fed into the lake. And with the full moon and stars shining so bright that night, the stream's running water caused thousands of tiny ripples on the surface. With the moon suspended above, the entire lake appeared to shimmer with thousands of silver flashes of moonbeams!

So we tied a couple of lures on our poles, and there we were, catching trout at midnight on Thousand Island Lake!

Scotty always loved to take things apart and put them back together. I remember when he completely dismantled his mother's alarm clock, springs, sprocket, screws, clappers, and all. He then proceeded to reassemble it. The sound of that alarm clock has never been the same!

Later in life, as Scott's depression grew unnoticed, we would find that Humpty-Dumpty didn't come with a lifetime warranty.

Have you ever tried to put a jigsaw puzzle together, only to find the last piece missing? You first become frustrated at the realization that all of your efforts seemed in vain.

Then you mourn a little for the unfinished masterpiece that could have been. But when you look at it again, you celebrate, not for what's missing, but what is left—it's beauty!

My son was a father to four children—two beautiful daughters and two wonderful sons—who I am so proud of and love very much.

Two months after Scott's disappearance, I received a call from the Mississippi detective that they discovered his body inside his car parked in a self-storage garage unit. He died from an apparent suicide.

It was determined that he had been dead for about two months. He died from carbon monoxide poisoning.

Now when I remember Scott, I can hear the words of Jesus as he told the parable of the lost sheep in Luke 15:4–7 NIV:

> Suppose one of you has a hundred sheep and loses one of them. Doesn't he leave the

23

ninety-nine in the wilderness and go after
the lost sheep until he finds it? And when he
finds it, he joyfully puts it on his shoulders
and goes home. Then he calls his friends
and neighbors together and says, 'Rejoice
with me; I have found my lost sheep. I tell
you that in the same way, there will be more
rejoicing in heaven over one sinner who
repents than over ninety-nine righteous
persons who do not need to repent.

The last note Scott left on earth was to God, asking for
forgiveness.

My son was found!

My mind continues its flashback in time to our nightly
ritual. I carried little Scotty upstairs on my shoulders, fireman's
carry style, and dropped him onto his bed. After a few minutes
of playful recaps on what happened during the day, I asked
him one final question, "Hey, Scotty, who's your best buddy?"

My mind is lost in the song's lyrics, "Watching Scotty
Grow" as I gaze at my sleeping boy safely tucked away in his
bed with our dog, Shilo, guarding his room.

And as my patio wind chimes softly transport me back
to reality, I hear Scotty's sleepy whisper, "You're my best
buddy, Dad."

> Though nothing can bring back the hour
> Of splendour in the grass
> of glory in the flower,
> We will grieve not, rather find,
> Strength in what remains behind.

> —William Wordsworth, "Splendour in the Grass"

TRACTORS WITH LUGS PROHIBITED

Don't burn bridges. You'll be surprised how many
times you have to cross the same river!

—Unknown

There is a scene in the movie, *It's a Wonderful Life*, where
George Bailey ends up on a bridge with thoughts of suicide.
A sign hangs at the entrance to the bridge.

It reads: "Tractors with lugs prohibited."

Most people think of lugs as the threaded stud that
holds the tire to the axle, an appendage that, when secured
by a lug nut, keeps the wheel from falling off.

But in George Bailey's case, the sign could have been a
warning for a man who might be going off his rocker. Just
when he is ready to jump into the icy waters and do away
with his life, his guardian angel, Clarence, appears to save the
day so that George does not harm himself.

George and Clarence had a symbiotic relationship.
Clarence wanted to earn his wings while George needed to
realize his worth.

Truth be told, the sign is actually for the benefit of the
bridge. Back in the nineteenth and twentieth centuries, farm
vehicles had lugs sticking out of their wheels. This bridge in

the movie most likely had a wooden floor, and tractor lugs would have torn up the bridge, making it impassable.

I think some people walk through life with their lugs on, never paying attention to the divots left behind, all the while ignoring the road signs posted in front of them.

When Moses came down from that mountain, he carried two stone tablets that contained ten directional signs etched into the granite to keep us on the straight and narrow.

Angels must shake their heads each time a human ignores these life-saving signs.

Road signs are everywhere.

Just yesterday as I drove to my neighboring town, I counted forty-seven of these chevrons along the way. One thing they all have in common is they warn us of what our future could be like without them.

Street signs come in all shapes and sizes, just like people. Sometimes signs are there to warn of impending danger. Some are telling us to change direction. And others are ordering us to stop in our tracks!

In 1400 BC, after wandering for forty years, the Israelites were camped on the banks of the Jordan River. They were poised to cross over and enter the Promised Land.

Egypt's domain was still significant to the south. The Hittites and Assyrians were gaining power in the North, and the Babylonians displayed their strength in the East.

And on that fertile riverbank, the Lord, through Moses, reinforced His first and greatest commandment.

In Deuteronomy 6:4–5 NIV, it states:

> Hear, O Israel! The Lord our God, the Lord is one. Love the Lord your God with all your heart and with all your soul and with all your strength.

Almost a millennium and a half later, while in the great temple in Jerusalem, Jesus complemented the greatest commandment with another, "Love your neighbor as yourself."

And with it, he provided the sandpaper to remove all the lugs from the human condition.

The next time you are down and out, ready to cross that bridge, proceed with caution and look for a sign.

Perhaps an angel might be hiding behind it, ready to point you in the right direction.

And if you are still carrying any lugs, seek out a neighbor and sand away!

Never drive faster than your guardian angel can fly!

—Unknown

TALE OF THE RAINBOWS

There is a fish in me... I know I came from salt
blue waters... I scurried with shoals of herring...
I blew waterspouts with porpoises...before
Noah...before the first chapter of Genesis.

—Carl Sandburg, "Wilderness"

It is late October, and the family is gone. The cabin is empty.
And I leave tomorrow. The Lord has richly blessed me. Now
it's time to bid goodbye to my boyhood place of wonder and
my son's remembrance tree. There was lots of laughter and
memorable moments with this gathering.

As I made my last cast, the mud hens and mallards
swim proudly by without disturbing my line. A lone western
wood duck dives under the water for a reed then surfaces and
makes his lonely *oo-eek* call, as if to say, "Where has everybody gone?"

And then the deer forage for food and water by the lake
as I take one last evening stroll. These silent creatures know
winter is approaching.

And as I look up to the heavens, I see the Orionids
meteor shower with the Milky Way serving as a ceiling in
God's giant cathedral, a thankful time in familiar places with
loved ones here in God's sanctuary.

Yes, the Lord has richly blessed me!

Seventy years ago, I threw out my fishing line into the great depths of Gull Lake. As my little bobber made its way over the ripples, my five-year-old mind imagined a monster rainbow taking my hook and line with me on the other end, giving it a fight that King David himself would have admired—no such luck!

Gull Lake is one of four bodies of water along the June Lake loop in the High Sierra Mountains. This scenic drive is part of the greater Mono Basin bordered by Yosemite National Park to the west and Nevada to the east.

The earliest inhabitants of this area were the Kucadikadi people. This band of Native Americans is part of the great Paiute nation.

While I'm sure these early tribesmen knew how to tempt a native trout out of Gull Lake, I am in awe that my fishing line has connected with many an ancestor of the Kucadikadi's bounty.

My life is tied forever to these colorful creatures!

I caught my first trout with my Langley fishing rod and reel that my uncle Louie gave me so many years ago. The pole came in two pieces. Although the top rod piece should have been oiled before it slid into the bottom half, my ten-year-old cousin Douglas dredged the pole piece through his butch-waxed hair and then inserted it to make my fishing rod complete.

Funny how certain rights of passage stick in your mind!

I can still feel the pull of that first "bow" as my rod tip bent to its limit. As the fish ran for its life, the drag on my reel sang out a tune that a Baptist choir would have envied.

My uncle and his friend Dominick were shouting words of encouragement.

"Play him, boy," yelled my uncle.

"Keep reeling, Larry," cried Dominick.

After what seemed an eternity, the fish and I saw each other eye to eye.

It was a beautiful sight!

I remember being camped by the shore of Gull Lake on a Friday with my uncle and Aunt Mildred; cousin Douglas; and their friends Dominic; wife, Ruth, and their daughters, Elaine and Linda.

Since I was the only practicing Catholic in the group, I abstained from eating meat on Fridays. This day was always tough because I would have trout with my hotcakes for breakfast, my spaghetti for lunch, and as my main course for dinner. You could say that trout was my food staple while vacationing in the mountains.

One particular Friday, I remember my uncle Louie grilling steaks on the campfire for everybody—that was the one time I really regretted my Friday fast.

The word Kucadikadi means "eaters of brine fly pupae," so I guess I can consider myself lucky in more ways than one!

Every time I see a rainbow after an Arizona monsoon storm, I remember the Kucadikadi people and the eyes of that first rainbow trout!

Many men go fishing all of their lives without
knowing that it is not the fish they are after.

—Henry David Thoreau

Day Two

God spoke, "Sky! In the middle of the waters; separate water from water! God made the sky. He separated the water under sky from the water above sky. And there it was, he named sky the Heavens. It was evening, it was morning—Day Two.

UNSINKABLE

Out of the night that covers me, Black as the
pit from pole to pole, I thank whatever gods
may be for my unconquerable Soul.
In the fell clutch of circumstance, I have not winced
nor cried out aloud. Under the bludgeonings of
chance My head is bloody, but unbowed.
Beyond this place of wrath and tears Looms but
the Horror of the shade, And yet the menace of
the years Finds and shall find me unafraid.
It matters not how strait the gate. How
charged with punishments the scroll,
I am the master of my fate; I am the captain of my soul.

—William Ernest Henley, "Invictus"

It was the summer of 1956. I was ten years old and a little
bored as I wandered around my new neighborhood. The first
friend I made was Mrs. Bacon. She was the ninety-year-old
mother of our neighbor who, each afternoon, sat in the shade
of Mr. Bacon's swing lounge chair on his front outdoor patio.

Visiting Mrs. Bacon was always fun because she made
me lemonade. As I petted her dog, Toby, she reminisced
about her younger days in New York City when she worked
as a telephone switchboard operator.

She said the summers in Los Angeles were very mild compared to New York. As she fanned herself, she told me that she had to wear a stuffy black dress for work with no hint of air conditioning. My lemonade suddenly tasted even colder!

This particular day, she was feeling sad for the forty-six passengers who just lost their lives in the collision of the ships *Andrea Doria* and *Stockholm*. She said it brought back memories of a friend of hers who died on the RMS Titanic forty-four years before.

Then she gazed past me as if in a trance and began to recite her memory. This former switchboard operator, now turned maritime radioman, was recounting when she first heard the fateful news:

> It was at seven bells when the ship struck the iceberg. There were over 2,200 passengers and crew on board. A little over two-and-a-half hours later, Titanic was gone. Fifteen hundred souls perished while a little over seven hundred survived.

Most of the survivors were first-class passengers who were lucky enough to be ushered on the lifeboats. The Titanic did not have enough lifeboats to accommodate all of its passengers, so those left behind had no option but to take their chances in the sea.

For those who were in the twenty-eight-degree water, death came very quickly as hypothermia led to heart and respiratory failure within ten to twenty minutes.

However what is astounding though is that out of the thousand plus who went into the frigid waters, forty survived!

I would say that those forty souls had resilience where the body's will to survive kicked in and punched death in the face, declaring, "Not here, not now, not at this moment!"

When you think all is lost and go beyond your limits, you will find resilience!

The prophet Isaiah knew this truth when he comforted the Israelites held captive in Babylon. In Isaiah 40:31 NIV, he declares, "But those who hope in the Lord will renew their strength. They will soar on wings like eagles; they will run and not grow weary, they will walk and not be faint."

A few months ago, during the Democratic primary presidential debate, the audience's final question was, "When did resilience carry you through a challenging time in your life?"

While some may have thought the question to be a softball, it allowed the candidates to share how they might lead 327 million Americans in uncertain times.

In a world of crisis and danger, resilience could be the most sought-after human quality that one would hope to keep in his or her pocket. Crusoe had his Friday, Rickenbacker had his seagull, and Columbus had his horizon.

People say that human skin starts out by having elasticity and the ability to stretch as the years go on. And as we age, our skin becomes paper-thin as we take on the scars of life. The process of surviving is when one truly knows what resilience is all about.

Resilience weaves itself throughout the social fabric of existence. It gives us our humanness. Only when our human strength serves out its term and leads us through life's labyrinth does it become a seed of hope for others to carry on in their lives.

Moses wrote so many years ago in Psalm 90:10 KJV:

The days of our lives are threescore and
ten; and if by reason of strength they
be fourscore years, yet is their strength
labour and sorrow; for it is soon cut off,
and we fly away.

As I sip my cold lemonade on this hot Arizona afternoon, I propose a toast: "Here's to you, Mrs. Bacon, as the
world turns, not here, not now, not at this moment!"

Hope itself is like a star—not to be seen in
the sunshine of prosperity and only to be
discovered in the night of adversity.

—Charles H Spurgeon

PUPPY DOGS' TAILS

What are little boys made of?
What are little boys made of?
Snips and snails
And puppy-dogs' tails
That's what little boys are made of
What are little girls made of?
What are little girls made of?
Sugar and spice
And everything nice
That's what little girls are made of.

—Robert Southey, "What Are Little Boys Made Of?"

My aunt Pat was a numismatist, lapidarist, philatelist, arctophile, and even a cagophilist. Yes, she was a connoisseur of coins, gems, stamps, teddy bears, and even keys.

Some people might call Aunt Pat a little eccentric, and others might call her colorful. I would describe her as a lady of wisdom with many talents. Every hobby that she took up got my attention, be it her collection of marbles, handmade elves, or even engraved leather craft.

Her hands were never idle. She left her mark whether she handcrafted cowboy hats, crocheted afghan blankets, or stitched Raggedy Ann dolls. She also taught me how to be an expert in seven card no peek poker, mah-jongg, and even the ancient game of knucklebones.

It was an adventure every time I came for a visit.

I remember getting into trouble with my father one day. Aunt Pat had a collection of matchbooks from all over the world. She kept them in a fishbowl on her coffee table. Yes, she was a phillumenist extraordinaire!

So at seven-years-old, I decided to start my own collection. As my friend and I ventured out on Sunset Boulevard, we found a whole crop of matchbooks littered on the sidewalk and street curbs. And they were free!

No one told us collectible matchbooks needed to be new and pristine. I thought they would look good inside my mother's mason jar. The problem was I had lost track of time and missed my doctor's appointment. When I got home, my father was livid.

I learned that day that the secret to collecting things is the item you find needs to be just as good on the inside as it is on the outside. You see, the soul has no worth unless it reflects its Maker's mark from the inside out.

From then on, I stuck to swapping marbles with my friends. Besides, aggies and cat's eyes were much more collectible in a boy's domain than worn out matchbooks!

Aunt Pat and my mother had a hard life growing up during the Great Depression. They never knew they were born to two different fathers until they became adults. Throughout their childhood, they were separated and boarded out to different homes in Maine.

Going without during hard times may explain why they collected things. Perhaps it is in the pursuit of collecting where we look for that one precious find throughout our lives. And when we discover it, we possess something that is of more value than all the gold on earth. Something that you will not find in a curio cabinet—something that is beyond monetary value.

The Bible says that we are made of dust. It tells us that God formed us by dust; and to dust, we will return. Jesus told the parable of the pearl of great price. He says that the kingdom of heaven is like a fine pearl. And as we seek to possess it, we should sell all that we have to own that one thing.

Interestingly, a pearl is formed from a little piece of dirt or grit, if you will. The gem starts out worthless, but then the oyster makes something of extreme value.

When I was about five years old, my cousin Carol, my sister Janet, and I played in Aunt Pat's backyard. As we sat on the grass, we started to get into a bit of an argument. The conversation drifted into a debate over who is smarter, a boy or a girl.

I was becoming frustrated as my two older foes teased me. I was losing the fight! As the discussion grew louder, I howled, "That's no fair, two against one!"

Out stepped Aunt Pat, assuming the role of referee. As she pulled me aside, she whispered, "Now you know, Larry, little boys are made of snakes, and snails, and puppy dogs' tails. And little girls are made of sugar and spice and everything nice."

Knowing I was within earshot, I whispered in Aunt Pat's ear, "I'll take the puppies!"

A few months later, Aunt Pat gave me a ceramic mug that she fired in her kiln. It sits in our curio cabinet between my wife's collection of Waterford and Swarovski.

The cup is painted with the images of a few puppies romping through the grass. One has floppy ears and a stubby crescent-shaped tail pointing to the sky. Another is sniffing at a snail hiding under a mushroom and another with his forepaws rigid and close to the ground, ready to skedaddle while he tries to entice a little snake out of his hole. All the while, butterflies and bees float around the wildflowers.

My Aunt Pat wrote a chapter in the book of life. Her pages are filled with a collection of things in life that should be celebrated and savored.

In the end, it is the stuff we are made of that counts!

In Matthew 5:13 NIV, Jesus concludes His Sermon on the Mount:

> You are the salt of the earth. But if the salt loses its saltiness, how can it be made salty again? It is no longer good for anything except to be thrown and trampled underfoot.

It is interesting to note that a human tear contains the same amount of salt as a drop of seawater. If we were to throw that drop back in the ocean, it would not make much difference. But when the salt that Jesus refers to becomes part of your spiritual makeup, we, as Christians, can make all the difference in the world.

Long before Sam Spade uttered his famous line about the Maltese Falcon, Prospero declared in Shakespeare's play, *The Tempest*, "We are such stuff as dreams are made on, and our little life is rounded with a sleep."

As I peer into our glass cabinet containing our life's treasures, I am reminded of the stuff that I am made of!

> When I was a child, I spoke like a child, I understood as a child, I thought as a child; but when I became a man, I put away childish things. For now we see in a mirror, dimly, but then face to face. Now I know in part, but then I shall know as I also am known.
>
> —1 Corinthians 13:11–12 NKJV

WHERE I'M BOUND

It is not down on any map, true places never are.

—Moby Dick, Herman Melville

I love to teach confirmation and Sunday school to the youth of our church. I have been doing it for over forty years. Most of the years, I would have the students write their faith statements where they share how their faith in God is working in their lives. The statement is usually in the form of an essay and read to the church. But every so often, I would propose to them, "Instead of writing a faith statement this year, why don't you plot your faith journey on a map?"

I would tell my students, "Now you have heard it said that the shortest distance between two points is a straight line. However a journey of faith doesn't happen that way. After all, a walk of faith is not on a level, well-manicured sidewalk. Oh no, the trip will have its ups and downs, mountains to climb, desert valleys to cross, and rushing rivers to forge. And all of it is on your walk of faith. Sometimes the trail is calm and serene with lakes to swim in and green pastures for respite. Then again, as you make your way through life, your road will have its twists and turns—places where your path is dark and seems to fall away. But when you think you can't go on, a light will shine in the darkness, and your road will become illuminated. You can count on it!"

Then I would show them a topographic map of Jesus's walk of faith, starting with a green pasture labeled "A Stable in Bethlehem" and ending on a jagged mountain pinnacle representing Golgotha with a cross on top.

I would tell them, "Your assignment is to plot your faith journey as if it were on a topographic map. And just as a topo map shows the contours of the land, you might want to draw flowered meadows and placid water pools to represent the happy and peaceful times in your life on this map. Maybe draw high rocky elevations or low desert valleys to show the trying times in your life."

So the students would draw their paths, each one different, as they shared their happiness with the birth of a brother or sister or a celebrated moment in their lives. And they would have their path climb some precipice to show the death of a loved one or their pet.

Then I would tell them, "Even though your path may not cross it, there are events happening in your world that, in some way, call out to your soul."

As my students plotted their map, it never ceased to amaze me as they considered what was happening in their world. Many of them drew waterfalls, desert oases and flowered meadows depicting great scientific and humanitarian achievements during their lifetime—the discovery of the internet, stem cell breakthroughs and the eradication of smallpox. Then they would draw some very different events with almost impassable terrain. Like the class of 2004 where on the side of their chart, they drew a landslide on a steep mountain slope and called it the Indian Ocean Tsunami where almost 230 thousand people were killed in a matter of a few minutes, 60 thousand of them children under the age of six!

Or the class of 1994 where they drew an arid desert with many images of bones. They called it Rwanda, a place where humans killed 800 thousand of their own kind!

Or the class of 2001…we all know what happened in September of that year!

Then there was the class of 1999. This class drew a jagged cliff. At the bottom of the cliff were the words "God Help Us All." Across the cliff's face was the word *Columbine!*

Oh yes, there is always pain and agony and suffering and human need on this world's horizon. I reminded my young confirmands about the words of John Kennedy's inaugural speech when he said, "The four common enemies of man are tyranny, poverty, disease, and war itself!"

Then I told them, "When it comes to your walk of faith, it will have many turns, and with each turn is a friend in need or maybe an enemy to be forgiven. And with each step you take, you take one step closer to God! As you take your walk of faith for the rest of your life, remember, because He said, 'It is finished,' you get to continue on your faith journey!"

When King David taught his son, Solomon, to follow Elohim's word and walk in his ways, he wrote in Psalm 119:105 KJV:

> Thy word is a lamp unto my feet
> and a light unto my path.

So take your walk seriously, folks. Remember others who don't necessarily cross your path. And those who do, well, remember our Lord's new commandment.

We all have our cross to carry as we make our way down life's trail. It always becomes more bearable when we keep His word within us as we walk!

What lies behind us and what lies ahead of us are
tiny matters compared to what lives within us.

—Ralph Waldo Emerson

GRANITE MOUNTAIN BECKONS

On the third new moon after the people of Israel had gone
out of the land of Egypt, on that day, they came into the
wilderness of Sinai. They set out from Rephidim and came
into the wilderness of Sinai, and they encamped in the
wilderness. There, Israel encamped before the mountain.

—Exodus 19:1–2 ESV

I live near the base of Granite Mountain in the high desert
area of Yavapai County in Arizona. The towns that surround
Granite Mountain include Prescott, Prescott Valley, and
Chino Valley to the east and Skull Valley and Yarnell to the
west and southwest.

As I sit and look at this mountain, I wonder what its
sculptor had in mind as his hands shaped it. Of course it
took millions of years to chisel its contours. This mountain
is not the tallest and certainly not the most prominent in the
scheme of early hills. But it has a calling to it just the same!

While I used to backpack in the mountains, I now love
to take late afternoon walks around sunset. It ranks right up
near the top of my daily pleasures of retirement. The route
that I take leads me on a trail where the pronghorn, javelina,
mountain lion, and coyote call home.

There is one bend on the path where Granite Mountain appears directly in your field of vision as you pass by. And from that vantage point, the sun sets right behind the mountain for a good portion of the year.

On this one particular day, low stratus clouds got between the setting of the sun and the mountain.

Granite Mountain seemed to be glowing!

For a moment, I thought to myself that I was looking at Mount Sinai. This foreboding mountain was sitting there in front of me with a fire sky backdrop!

Granite Mountain and Mount Sinai are very much alike. Their faces have the same contours. Mount Sinai consists of granite. So does Granite Mountain. Mount Sinai sits in a desert. You will also find Granite Mountain in a desert. Mount Sinai has an elevation of 7,500 feet. Granite Mountain has an altitude of 7,600 feet.

And when I got home and checked the world weather report, I was amazed. At that moment, the top of Mount Sinai had a temperature of forty-one degrees with twenty-miles-per-hour winds out of the west. And the top of Granite Mountain? It was forty-one degrees with twenty-miles-per-hour winds out of the west!

Then I wondered, what could have been on the minds of those ancient Israelites as they camped at the base of Mount Sinai in the late fourteenth century BC? The Bible tells us they were in awe and fear. Maybe they feared what their future would be? Maybe they wondered what God had in store for them?

And then I pondered, what about those who reside at the base of Granite Mountain? As modern-day descendants of ancient humanity, maybe we, too, live in awe and fear. Perhaps we fear what our future will be. Maybe my neighbors are asking, what does God have in store for us?

Well those ancient Israelites left their Mount Sinai encampment and roamed the land for forty years until some finally found the Promised Land.

But what about those of us who still reside here at the base of Granite Mountain? What about our promised land?

I think our promised land is right here, in this place, at this time, in this moment!

Jesus told us not to worry about the future. He told us in Matthew 6:25, 32–34 ESV:

> Therefore I tell you, do not be anxious about your life, what you will eat, or what you will drink, nor about your body, what you will put on. Is not life more than food, and the body more than clothing?" "For the Gentiles seek after all these things, and your heavenly Father knows that you need them all. But seek first the kingdom of God and his righteousness, and all these things will be added to you. Therefore do not be anxious about tomorrow, for tomorrow will be anxious for itself. Sufficient for the day is its own trouble.

But the path to the future and righteousness can be frightening even after Jesus gave His disciples words of comfort.

In John 14:4–6 NIV, he says, "'You know the way to the place where I am going.' Thomas said to him, 'Lord, we don't know where you are going, so how can we know the way?' Jesus answered, 'I am the Way and the Truth and the Life. No one comes to the Father except through me.'"

In the meantime, in this place, at this moment, there is work to be done in this promised land.

So take up your cross and make disciples of others. Baptize and teach them. Welcome strangers, feed the hungry, clothe the naked, care for the sick, and oh yes, visit the imprisoned, whatever their imprisonment may be.

I've realized at my age, I can say with certainty, I have seen more yesterdays than I will ever see tomorrows on this earth. And if I can, I'd like to leave this promised land with the etiquette of a good backpacker: Leave the place you traveled just a little better than you found it!

The Promised Land always lies on the
other side of a wilderness.

—Havelock Ellis

PLANES, TRAINS, AND AUTOMOBILES

New friends may be poems, but old friends are
alphabets. Don't forget the alphabets because
you will need them to read the poems.

—William Shakespeare

This past year has been a memorable one as I took my journey of faith literally. You might even call it a story of "biblical proportion" as it lasted forty days and forty nights. The trip covered over five thousand miles across twenty states. It was a journey that added a deeper appreciation of my faith with humility, prayer, gratitude, love, and even a twinge of courage.

I've always been comfortable traveling alone. I mean the majority of times when I traveled on business, I was by myself. Before my son was old enough and after our kids had families of their own, I backpacked alone in the High Sierras. But this trip was different. I was traveling by myself first class in luxury with a private room on a train.

The purpose of my trip was simple: visit the people and places my wife used to ask me to when we made our road trips in the past. Somehow, time always got in the way and we never got around to it. The idea was to see friends, family, and extended family along the way with three modes of transportation; planes, trains, and automobiles.

My "party of one" departed at sunrise from Flagstaff, Arizona, by a train bound for Chicago. A few miles down the track, we passed by the town of Winona. I couldn't help but think of the lyrics to Bobby Troupe's song "Route 66" where he names the more famous cities along the highway and then reminds us, "Don't forget Winona!" Funny how those who made their way from Chicago to LA would rush by this little town with no thought of notoriety.

As I peered out my train roomette window, I had to laugh at myself as one who pays to travel in luxury now finding himself stuck on this passenger train, playing second fiddle to a freight train. You see, all passenger trains need to pull over to a sidetrack when a freight train steams past.

Then I wondered, could humility be taking priority by stepping in when others might be in more need than me? Who knows what a freight car's treasure might be? Perhaps it's home to a lonely vagabond, wishing America good morning.

Wouldn't this world be a better place if we all stopped along the way to help another neighbor who is sidetracked in life?

As we crossed into Illinois from Iowa, we stopped after getting word that another freight became derailed ahead of us. So our engineer put the locomotives in reverse, and we backtracked forty miles to the Iowa border. We then switched track and took another route to Chicago.

All the passengers became a little closer that night as our conversations were that of consoling sojourners. There was a day when I would have been frustrated at the thought of canceling some profitable business appointment. But today this little delay just added to my adventure.

The observation car was full of philosophical lament as we limped along fifteen hours behind schedule. I dozed off only to be awakened by a familiar screech followed by an abrupt final jolt. The clock inside Union Station showed it was three o'clock in the morning.

After getting a few hours of sleep at the Hyatt Place a few blocks from Union Station, I drove to South Bend, Indiana, to see the University of Notre Dame. I have always been intrigued by Notre Dame. I'm not sure if it was the calling of the classroom or the cathedral.

Perhaps the two forces that leads one to wisdom is the light of knowledge coupled with the spirit of faith. This was just the place where I wanted to be!

I ended my campus tour that evening at the Our Lady of the Lourdes grotto. This place reflects such serenity in the glow of the candlelight. My thoughts turned to my wife and son's memory as I knelt in prayer and placed two candles among the hundreds of flickering lights.

Suddenly I realized that I wasn't alone as Robert Browning Hamilton's poem came to my mind:

> I walked a mile with Pleasure;
> She chatted all the way;
> But left me none the wiser
> For all she had to say.
>
> I walked a mile with Sorrow;
> And ne'er a word said she;
> But, oh! The things I learned from her
> When Sorrow walked with me.

As the candles flickered, I learned that gratitude illuminated this sanctuary and gave me faith with an even deeper meaning that evening.

I went to visit with Wendy's ninety-two-year-old grandaunt in Indianapolis. Velma was a remarkable lady. She lived through WWII, the great depression, and all things historical in the country since. But history takes a back seat to her. She was sharp as a tack. It was a challenge to keep up with her when it came to sports statistics—be it basketball, boxing, or even her beloved Indy Colts.

I stayed with her son and his family and got a chance to see the Indy 500 up close and personal.

I drove on to West Virginia to visit with three of my adult grandkids and four of my new great-grandchildren. Joy filled my heart as I sat in the center of a family photo with my third and fourth generation children. I felt like Father Abraham as I posed with them for a photo. Could you imagine what a fantastic family portrait his would have been!

Five days later, I continued to Pennsylvania to reunite with a high school friend I hadn't seen in forty-five years. Instantly, a thousand questions and memories dominated the conversation like cruising down Route 1A in my '57 Chevy, weekends at Thompson Lake in Maine, and homework assignments in English literature, comparing notes on the works of John Donne.

As we relived our school days, we remembered the exact moment in class when Oswald's bullet struck President Kennedy, and the days spent lamenting how the world seemed to be turned upside down with riots, drugs and chaos at the start of the Vietnam War.

As our visit came to a close, we agreed that forty-five years is too long a pause for two old friends to get together as we bid goodbye. We both had to admit that God uses people to brighten this world. After all, *no man is an island!*

I continued on to NYC for the weekend and had dinner with my grandson and his wife, then on to New England to spend time with more friends and family.

I stayed with Wendy's best friend and her husband, visited with our old friends, former church members in New Hampshire, and took my goddaughter to a Red Sox game.

I then flew to Florida and spent a little time with my son and his wife. After a week, I drove through Alabama and Mississippi. I stayed and celebrated in the French Quarter of New Orleans, dining on jambalaya and strolling down the rues. I watched the faces of those mesmerized by trumpets and saxophones as they listened to jazz and the blues.

I drove through Texas where I stayed next door to the Alamo. While there, I imagined what it was like for that small Texan group fighting to hold on to their home. I wondered about their faith as they each died for their cause.

The bullet-ridden walls reminded me that faith sometimes takes a lot of courage. As they stood guard on the top of those walls, perhaps the words of Psalm 27 KJV may have comforted them: "The Lord is my light and my salvation. Whom shall I fear?"

Finally, when I crossed from New Mexico to Arizona, I had to pull off the highway. A giant dust storm engulfed the road, causing all traffic to come to a halt. They call it a haboob and tell you to pull over, turn off your lights, and don't touch the brake pedal to avoid a collision from behind.

As I sat in the dark with the outside raging, I thought of Jesus praying in the garden just before his crucifixion.

He told his disciples in John 14:27 NIV:

> My peace I leave you; my peace I give you. I do not give to you as the world gives. Do not let your hearts be troubled, and do not be afraid.

Just then, the outside quieted, and the darkness turned to light, and I knew my journey had come to an end. I was home!

> It is always hard to see the purpose in wilderness wanderings until they are over.

—John Bunyan, *Pilgrim's Progress*

SEDONA SUNRISE

For you shall go out in joy and be led forth in peace; the mountains and the hills before you shall break forth into singing, and all the trees of the field shall clap their hands.

—Isaiah 55:12 NIV

I took a hike today in the early morning hours before the sun's rays begin to peek through the canyon walls of Sedona. At sixty-five degrees with no wind, the weather was just about perfect.

The only noise I could hear was an occasional call of a yellow-headed blackbird. To the west, I hear the sound of a hot-air balloon's burner hissing away as this colorful airship ascends into the clear blue sky.

The balloon appears to be like a modern-day deco painting with a vivid patchwork of reds, purples, blues, and yellows hung in suspension on the horizon. Then it is followed by a dozen or more ascending crafts. One adorned with black-and-yellow spots that would make a bumblebee blush. The others decked out with an assortment of rainbow colors. All of them have already got a glimpse of my sunrise to come.

I sit on my perch opposite Cathedral Rock as I start to see the approach of dawn's twilight. I have been here for a little over an hour. Sailors would call this time nautical dawn as the sun is still twelve degrees below the horizon. The surrounding rocks still have a dark charcoal profile as they wait for the sun's brush to blossom them into color.

As I wait with anticipation, I imagine how this whole area was once at the sea's bottom. And after hundreds of millions of years, the sea sacrificed the remains of billions of sea creatures and shells to become a palette rich with God's colors as Father Time painted the limestone with iron oxide on the rocks that I sit on now.

I'm sure that when the two coasts of the Pangaea collided and launched the mighty Rockies, it caused this place to bloom with a million sights to behold.

I think back to watching television on Christmas Eve in 1968. Three days earlier, three humans in Apollo 8 left the earth's pull to orbit another heavenly body for the first time in humankind's history.

As Astronaut William Anders took the very first photo of our planet from the Lunar Orbiter, it was a fantastic sight to behold.

It was the first earthrise humanity had ever seen!

It was a beautiful blue marble with white wisps of clouds clinging to our domain and suspended in space. The memory of that sight kind of put the hot air balloons above me to shame!

Our earth, with its blue green hues, gives off a soft, tranquil look. Is it any wonder that a little over seven months after the Apollo 8 mission, Neil Armstrong stepped out on the moon's surface in a place called the Sea of Tranquility?

The crew of Apollo 11 left our calling card to other visitors, declaring that "We came in peace!" I ask myself if visitors from another world would agree with that decree after making mankind's acquaintance?

The first ray of our sun's light has reached my eyes now, and morning has broken. It never ceases to amaze me that each new sunrise is spectacular and unique in its own beauty.

If they were to name the seven wonders of the world for places of peace, this spot would be my nomination!

> We do not describe the world we see, we
> see the world we can describe.

—Rene Descartes

Day Three

God spoke, "Separate! Water beneath Heaven, gather into one place; Land, appear!" And there it was. God named the land Earth. He named the pooled water Ocean. God saw that it was good.

God spoke, "Earth, green up! Grow all varieties of seed-bearing plants, every sort of fruit-bearing tree." And there it was. Earth produced green seed-bearing plants, all varieties, and fruit-bearing trees of all sorts. God saw that it was good. It was evening, it was morning—Day Three.

LITTLE WENDY AND THE FIVE QUESTIONS

Children are the hands by which we take hold of heaven.

—Henry Ward Beecher

My five-year-old granddaughter, Little Wendy, and I have a daily ritual. When I am seated in my recliner, she comes up to me at the end of the day. I used to ask her, "What did you do today?" And I would get a brief reply, "I played and had fun"—end of story!

Now I am seated in my recliner, staring at the flames in my fireplace. I look over to see little Wendy propping up a cardboard box cutout reminiscent of a child's lemonade stand. At the top of the box are the words 'Wendy's news.' With pad and pencil in hand, she declares that she wants to be a news reporter. She anticipates my usual question and tells me that she just made a preschool friend that day and wants to write a story about him.

She then asks me, "But how do I write my story, Papa?" As she poses her question, I think of the old Chinese proverb:

A child's life is like a piece of paper on
which every person leaves a mark!

After explaining what the word journalism means, I remind her that she has to learn how to read and write first! Then I tell her, "When I was in school, my teacher taught me that the first thing you need to do in journalism is always get the answer to the five questions: Who? What? Where? When? and How? When you do that, you will always have a story.

And then I told her, "Later, you might include the answer to the sixth and final question: Why? But let's not include the answer to this question for now."

Little Wendy presses me, "But why can't I include that question, Papa?"

"Well," said I, "If you answer that question, sometimes you will have others who may disagree with your answer. They might even say your story is fake. They might not want to call you a friend and may even say you are an enemy."

I explained to her what the difference is between a fact and an opinion. I tell her, "Sometimes your answer may not come from the facts but your opinion. And when that happens, people can react very differently."

I continue, "Remember, when you tell a story about someone, it always is best to get to know that person well before talking about them. It might be best to leave the sixth question unanswered, for now, and stay friends for as long as you can. For there will be many more places and many more people and many, many more friends to become stories in your life!"

As to the *why*, well we'll save that one for a little later!

My child, hold on to your wisdom and insight. Never let them get away from you. They will provide you with life—a pleasant and happy life. You can go safely on your way and never even stumble. You will not have to worry about sudden disasters as come on the wicked like a storm. The Lord will keep you safe. He will not let you fall into a trap. Whenever you possibly can, do good to those who need it.

—Proverbs 3:21–27 GNT

IF TREES COULD TALK

A seed hidden in the heart of an apple
is an orchard invisible.

—A Welsh Proverb

I have a friend; her name is Patty. Whenever we end our conversation, she bids me goodbye with "You're a good man, Charlie Brown." So I couldn't resist but to respond to her with "Until we talk again, Peppermint Patty."

Now there have been many times when Charles Shultz placed Charlie Brown and Peppermint Patty under an apple tree discussing a range of subjects from the meaning of life, to love, and even to their faith in humanity.

Apples and trees have been part of the human conversation ever since man uttered his first words. Adam and Eve started the conversation with the breaking of a rule. And ever since, our discussions have taken us in all directions except up.

Legend has it that Sir Isaac Newton was sitting under a tree when he got clobbered on the head by a falling apple. Hence, among the other discoveries of the universe's laws, he discovered the law of gravity. I guess it pays to look up for your own safety!

After all, isn't laying in the grass under a tree's shade on a hot afternoon just about the best place to have a heart-to-heart conversation? I mean, you're relaxed and comfortable, the stresses of life seem to have momentarily melted away, and you are looking up!

I once gave an assignment to my confirmation students. I asked them to choose a tree that came closest to representing their walk of faith.

Katie chose the Bristlecone pine tree. She said Bristlecone pines are among the oldest trees on earth. There is one called Methuselah that grows in the Bristlecone Pine Forest in California, a little northwest of Death Valley.

Although the Bible says that Methuselah, the man, died at 969 years old, this living tree is almost five thousand years old! What stories of wisdom would await us if this ancient tree could talk?

Katie, as you go through life, may your stories grow and may you walk forever faithful!

Sam chose a baobab tree. Here is a tree that grows on the African plains. Some baobabs are said to have lived over 1,500 years. With its Medusa-like branches, natives have dubbed this tree to be the Tree of Life.

I could imagine two Maasai tribesmen crouching under a baobab tree with their spears adorned in lion fur and impala hide, having a conversation about the circle of life as they look out on the Serengeti horizon.

Sam, you, as everyone in our class, are a child of God. May your faith be adorned with uniqueness and strength!

There is a tree that proudly grows near the 9/11 reflecting pools in the middle of ground zero. In October of 2001, when the autumn colors bid goodbye to the foliage and one month after the twin towers came crashing down, rescue workers discovered a few green leaves sprouting out of a twisted tree branch.

They found the branch connected to a charred stump buried in the ashes of death and destruction. This decapitated Callery Pear Tree endured the collapse of more than 1.8 million tons of debris.

Today its new boughs bear pure white flower blossoms celebrating new life. And, while the scar of terrorism and evil remain within humankind, the rings of this tree's wood cells tell us a story of hope and survival.

Perhaps if the world were an orchestra pit, and the trees were the musicians, they would play the most delightful overture every spring and every fall, they would conclude with their heavenly lullaby.

Yes, I think this world would be just a little more beautiful if trees could talk!

I frequently tramped eight or ten miles through the deepest snow to keep an appointment with a beech tree or a yellow birch or an old acquaintance among the pines.

—Henry David Thoreau, *Walden*

THE WROUGHT
IRON SETTEE

"If you want to touch the past, touch a rock.
If you want to touch the present, touch a flower.
If you want to touch the future, touch a life."

—Unknown

The year was 1955. My beloved Brooklyn Dodgers won their first World Series. *The $64,000 Question* and *Lassie* dominated TV. The first McDonald's restaurant opened its doors, and Elvis signed with Colonel Parker to launch his singing career.

Life was good as my friends and I donned our Davy Crockett coonskin caps. The "happiest place on earth" opened in Anaheim, California, and I was a card-carrying member of the Mickey Mouse Club.

It felt like an adventure as this nine-year-old stepped into a magic kingdom. It was as though Disney's television show came to life complete with heroes and villains. At the time, the park consisted of the four lands of Adventure, Frontier, Fantasy, and Tomorrow.

Disneyland had only thirty-six attractions during that first year. They sold a book with tickets that were designated with *A* through *C* attraction values. An *A* ticket had a cost of ten cents with a *C* ticket value of a quarter. The famous *E* ticket attraction didn't come until four years later with the arrival of the Matterhorn, Submarine, and Monorail attractions.

For the next sixty years, I would frequently return to the park. Some years I would have an annual pass where I would stop by on my way home from work. I would also entertain clients as my industry would once a year exclusively take over the park for a few hours in the evening.

Of all the attractions I enjoyed with my children and grandchildren, my favorite time didn't require an *A* ticket or even an *E* ticket. It was merely sitting on a wrought iron settee on Main Street near the park entrance.

The settee was positioned so you could see the faces of every subject of the Magic Kingdom as they passed by. Did you know that it can take up to twenty-six muscles in the human face to express a smile? Whenever I sat on that settee, I saw faces using all their muscles! Faces full of wonder and amazement, gleeful cherub-like faces caught in a happy trance as though they had just entered through the children's gates of heaven.

I don't believe I counted one unhappy face during the entire time I sat on that chair throughout the years. It was almost as if you could understand all of the more than one hundred languages spoken by children to their parents as they walked down Main Street.

It always seemed that the parents received every one of their children's comments with laughter and joyful looks as they passed by. And as I watched families of every color and creed speaking in their native tongue, I think I could have served as a park interpreter as one who is fluent in the smile language. It reminded me of Art Linkletter's old show, *Kids Say the Darndest Things*.

I think the settee served as a refuge; a place where you could sit and observe our brothers and sisters in their natural state of happiness. Funny how so many of God's children seem to go unnoticed as they parade through life on their way to His kingdom.

In Luke's gospel, Jesus tells us that our God has His eye on every creature on earth. In Luke 12:6–7 NIV, he says:

> Are not five sparrows sold for two pennies? Yet not one of them is forgotten by God. Indeed the very hairs on your head are numbered. Don't be afraid; you are worth more than many sparrows.

Later, in the gospel, Jesus is asked by the Pharisees when the kingdom of heaven would come. In Luke 17:20–21 NIV, he says:

> The coming of the kingdom of God is not something that can be observed, nor will people say, 'Here it is,' or 'There it is,' because the kingdom of God is in your midst.

And yet perhaps it is what we give and what we do with what has been provided for us that shines in front of our Lord and the angels.

As recorded in Mark 12:41–44 NIV:

> Jesus sat down opposite the place where offerings were put and watched the crowd putting their money into the temple treasury. Many rich people threw in

large amounts. But a poor widow came and put in two very small copper coins worth only a few cents.

Calling his disciples to him, Jesus said, "Truly I tell you, this poor widow has put more into the treasury than all the others. They gave out of their wealth; but she, out of her poverty, put everything—all she had to live on."

Sometimes the cheapest attractions in life can become the most rewarding of adventures. In a way, the wrought iron settee was the best ride in the park. And you weren't required to keep your hands and arms and legs inside the vehicle at all times.

All you had to do was sit back and watch the parade go by!

If you want happiness for an hour, take a nap.
If you want happiness for a day, go fishing.
If you want happiness for a year, inherit a fortune.
If you want happiness for a lifetime, help somebody!

—Chinese Proverb

LET IT BE

He had a dream in which he saw a stairway, resting
on the earth, with its top reaching to heaven, and the
angels of God were ascending and descending on it.

—Genesis 28:12 NIV

There is a beautiful fable about Egypt and Egyptian heaven.
When an Egyptian dies, his soul ascends to the gates of
heaven. There, a gatekeeper has two questions for him. The
answers to which will determine whether or not he will get
into heaven.

The first question is, "Have you had joy in your life?"
The second question is, "Have you given joy to others?"

Joy must have been sprinkled in that dust when God
formed man. I think it's part of our genetic makeup. It's the
one human ingredient that must be shared with others in
order to see its radiance.

Last week in church, the gospel for the day was about
the Transfiguration of our Lord. Jesus and His disciples,
Peter, James, and John, are on this high mountain. The gospel records how the three disciples were in awe when they
saw Jesus shining in dazzling white with Moses and Elijah
standing next to him against the mountain's shadow.

As our pastor read the gospel story, I thought of the
movie, *Blinded by the Light*, where a Pakistani youth tries to

find his way in life, living in London's suburbs. He becomes intrigued by Bruce Springsteen's lyrics to his song, "Blinded by the Light." The teen's inspiration shows his pure joy of music and art through his songs and poetry. His own creativity then touches the lives of many souls in his neighborhood.

Peter, James, and John were, if you will, blinded by the light of joy, for a moment, upon that mountainside. Peter didn't want to leave the place. He even wanted to build three tabernacles at that spot so each apparition could dwell there forever. He sought to have "joy tapped in a tabernacle!"

Of course God stepped in, and Peter and friends came down from that place to climb mountains of their own.

We started a ministry in our church called the Traveling Bible Group. It consists of a group of members who go out to anyone who wants to have a Bible study or just a little companionship.

We visit those who can't travel to church—souls confined to their hospital room, hospice bed, or prison cell. It can be something special when one can take a few steps with another as they continue on their soul's journey home.

Marie was in her nineties and a member of our church, living with her granddaughter instead of a hospice house. Whenever I visited Marie alone, her ever faithful calico cat, Patches, would sit on Marie's pillow purring. When I visited with others, Patches would peer at us through a crack in the closet door.

It was a pleasure to spend time with Marie. She was always upbeat and looked forward to our time together. There she was, sitting in her bed, with a large bay window behind her. Every time I visited her, I could see the willows in the foreground with the Mingus Mountains in the distance. The sunlight flooded through the glass, giving Marie a halo effect.

She loved the hymn, "On Eagle's Wings." Each time we saw her, she would pull out her hymnal from the nightstand and ask us to sing it a cappella.

When I asked her, "In your long life, what was the most beautiful sight you have seen?" She paused for a moment then said, "I remember seeing a condor soaring on a Sunday afternoon in the Grand Canyon."

You could see the joy on her face as she continued her recollection, "Although the condor doesn't have the beauty of an eagle, this one sailed through the air with all the grace and majesty that God intended!"

She said she felt a little guilty that day because she missed the church service. As we left, we agreed that Marie enjoyed a spiritual moment that went far beyond what any human-made cathedral could offer!

Marie passed away peacefully a few weeks later.

I did not know Mary like others in our church, but I am so grateful for the visits I had with her in her hospice room. The room was at the rear of the house, so you couldn't help but be greeted by other residents as you made your way through the living room, kitchen, and hallway.

I always loved to call on Mary because she was the perfect hostess. On one visit, before taking a drink, Mary offered me a drink from her spill-proof cup. But that was Mary, always putting others first, even in her suffering! I think she was the heart and soul of our church's interfaith meal ministry that served so many in our community.

Mary was a sixty-eight-year-old grandmother of six. The lung disease had taken its toll as she needed round-the-clock care. During my first visit, I got the chance to learn how much of a Beatles fan Mary was. She told me that she was thirteen when she saw them make their American debut on *The Ed Sullivan Show*.

When I asked her what her favorite Beatles song was, her facial features softened as she replied, "Let It Be"! I heard that Paul McCartney wrote that song as a tribute to his mother, Mary, who died from cancer when Paul was fourteen.

Mary's room speaks of Christmas! It has a giant snowflake above her bed. There are a couple of Christmas trees on the shelf below her and ornaments everywhere.

When I asked Mary, "What was the most beautiful sight you ever saw in your life?" she pointed to the collage of pictures hanging at the end of her bed and said, "Right there, my grandchildren's faces."

On my last visit, when I was ready to leave, I whispered to Mary, "Maybe Paul had you in mind too, Mary, when he wrote the lyrics to your favorite song."

Mary passed away a few days later.

I guess the stairway to heaven has many flights. And in between each flight is a landing. And maybe you're lucky enough to have a conversation with your fellow pilgrims while catching your breath on that landing. And during those precious chats, you will always find some joy!

And as that pilgrim continues to climb past you until he or she is out of sight, don't worry, just let it be!

> Joy lies in the fight, in the attempt, in the suffering involved, not in the victory itself.
>
> —Mahatma Gandhi

DEM BUMS

Tyger, tyger, burning bright,
In the forest of the night;
What immortal hand or eye,
Could frame thy fearful symmetry?

—William Blake, "The Tyger"

A voice from the back porch of my memories crackles over my transistor radio. It declares, "It's time for Dodger baseball!" I see an image of my glove hanging on my bedroom wall as I imagine myself standing in a stretch position on the mound at Dodger Stadium. By now the Dodgers have won two World Series, and I am focused on graduating high school bound for a New England college.

The voice jogs my memory, and I go further into time as I think of two matches burning bright on a chilly LA night when my father and I held them up to join ninety-three thousand other flickering points of light. We were seated way out behind the left-center fence in the peristyle end of the coliseum. It was a school night, Thursday, May 7, 1959.

The Dodgers were hosting the New York Yankees in an exhibition game. We were spectators in the largest crowd in baseball history. The game paused momentarily when Pee Wee Reese pushed paraplegic Roy Campanella in his wheelchair out to home plate. Campy was only thirty-six years old when a near-fatal car accident ended his all-star career.

My glove then segues me back further in time as I remember how thrilled I was when I heard that the Brooklyn Dodgers were moving to my home town. I was nine years old when the team won their first World Series in their history that began in 1883. And to me, a west coast boy who loved baseball, it was even sweeter because the Brooklyn Dodgers defeated the dreaded New York Yankees!

Although we had no major league team in LA at the time, my father and I would playfully argue over who was the better team. And every time I brought up the Dodgers, he would reply, "Who dem bums?" A phrase that so many disappointed Brooklynites used throughout the years of losing to the crosstown Bronx Bombers.

My mother worked days in retail, and my father worked nights as a bartender. So I rarely saw him except for his days off. Whatever conversations, we had always seemed to converge around baseball. And the Dodgers always gave us something to talk about.

Whenever we were lucky enough to go to a game, it was as if we entered into a different land. The spectators who sat near us became neighbors of one accord. Whether it was clapping our hands, stomping our feet, or shouting our sentiments to the home plate umpire, we were one!

It seemed as if every other fan in the stadium had a transistor radio. And when the buzzing of the crowd noise toned down, you could hear the voice of Vin Scully echoing throughout the ballpark.

It was the way he painted a picture with words for each player at the plate or on the mound, be it friend or foe. "Stargell is standing on the left side of the plate, his bat pinwheeling in anticipation of the pitch." or "Koufax, pausing on the mound, blowing on his hand, he looks in to get the sign. He winds up, right leg reaching for the stars, and he fires. Fastball swung on and missed!" Or Vinny would describe another event about to happen as the crowd chants, "Go, go, go!"

"Wills takes his lead from first, there he goes. He dives headfirst. Safe!"

Robert Gordon was born in the Philippines in 1909. He came down with polio when he was a child. The disease left him with a slight limp for the rest of his life. Before meeting my mother in Boston, he sailed around the world several times as a merchant seaman.

During World War II, he worked as a welder at the Long Beach Naval Shipyard. Several years later, he contracted tuberculosis when I was in junior high school. The asbestos in the shipyard may have led to the disease. When diagnosed, the LA County Health Department ordered him out of our house to a place called Olive View Sanitarium in Sylmar, California. He would remain there for the next two years.

Tuberculosis has claimed its victims throughout much of known history. According to the CDC, by the beginning of the nineteenth century, TB killed one out of every seven humans living in the United States and Europe.

And the stigma of this hideous illness continued through the twentieth century. And it was always fuel for schoolyard prejudice and bullying.

Olive View consisted of several wooden buildings nestled in a hot, dry area of the San Fernando Valley. My father was added to the many resident patients who were sick, suffering, and dying.

The staff placed him next to the patio door of his ward. It overlooked a field of olive trees. To this day, I am amazed at the thought that Jesus and His disciples chose to stay on a mountain of olives while my father and other sufferers dwelled in a valley of olives!

I remember having to stand on the grass outside of his ward during our weekly visits. The conversation still revolved around "Dem Bums." He returned home and resumed his bartending job when I started high school.

On my twenty-third birthday, when my wife, mother, and I went to share a moment to see my father accept his award at the International Bartenders Competition at the Beverly Hilton, he suffered a heart attack and died shortly after that.

He was fifty-nine years old.

To this day, the crack of a bat hitting a ball or the smell of peanuts and hot dogs or the voice of the greatest announcer in baseball history brings me to a place of serenity and the memory of two matches burning bright in the night sky!

> When I was a boy of fourteen, my father was so ignorant. I could hardly stand to have the old man around. But when I got to be twenty-one, I was astonished at how much he had learned in seven years!
>
> —Mark Twain

THE CALL OF NEW ENGLAND

Two roads diverged in a yellow wood,
And sorry I could not travel both
And be one traveler, long I stood
And looked down one as far as I could
To where it bent in the undergrowth;

I shall be telling this with a sigh
Somewhere ages and ages hence:
Two roads diverged in a wood, and I—
I took the one less traveled by,
And that has made all the difference.

—Robert Frost, "The Road Not Taken"

Legend has it that Peter Pan and his Wendy flew around London's Big Ben clock to get their bearings as they set their course for Neverland.

The chimes of this chronometer declare its preciseness with every tick of time, a pulse so steady that it has become the gold standard for timekeeping. And to this day, it could be argued that every train conductor throughout the world sets his pocket watch by Big Ben's cadence.

I boarded the City of Los Angeles as it pulled away from Union Station. I was seventeen, and my life was about to change forever. As the train chugged down the track, Martin Luther King addressed the nation with his "I Have A Dream" speech.

I remember hearing MLK's words on a radio while on a short stop in Green River, Wyoming. Each time I read the words of Isaiah, I hear MLK bellowing out: "I have a dream that one day, every valley shall be exalted, every hill and mountain shall be made low, the rough places will be made plain, the crooked places shall be made straight, and the glory of the Lord shall be revealed, and all flesh shall see it together."

Conversations in the domed lounge car centered around MLK's inspiring words as the sun disappeared in the purple Nebraska sky.

New England was my final destination as I was bound for this magical place where the air was crisp and the colors of my future set in promise. I would be living with my aunt and uncle in the quaint town of Walpole, Massachusetts.

It was my senior year of high school: new place, new friends, new life! But culture shock set in as I realized my new found world spoke in a different language.

I attended my first Walpole High School football game. It was their homecoming game with neighboring Norwood High School. As the teams competed, I found myself seated with the Norwood students.

As I watched their cheerleaders shouting through their megaphones, I heard them yell, "Give me an *N*," and the kids yelled, "*N*!"

"Give me an *O*," and the kids yelled, "O!"

"Give me an *R*," then the entire bleachers erupted with "Ahhh!"

Even my teachers spoke with this foreign accent. Why, the president himself talked their language. During the Cuban missile crisis, I remember JFK briefing our nation about the Russian missiles in "Cuber."

It was 1963, Walpole and LA were two worlds within me. "Dem Bums" swept the Yankees in the World Series. Koufax and Drysdale ruled LA, but the colors of a New England fall captured my awe.

I found that New Englanders had a sense of warmth that I never knew. Everyone seemed to know everyone. My roots came from Hollywood, where the woods consisted of palm trees and asphalt, a clambake was a grunion run, and a lobster roll took the form of a fish taco!

Two months into my school year, a moment happened where everyone in our school would remember exactly where they were as a shot rang out in Dallas.

For the next few days, with the foliage almost gone, Boston no longer glowed with its brilliance. As I walked through the common the day after the shooting, it seemed as if the world became veiled in gray and black.

It wasn't long until the blackness turned to white with a freeze and then the snow. My newfound friends thought I was a little crazy as the kid from California marveled at a frozen sidewalk puddle while he slid by in his street shoes.

I skated on the frozen lake across the road. New Pond was the gathering place for the local youth, and the kids taught me the game of ice hockey.

My senior year ended with pomp and circumstance as I dated our class valedictorian. We celebrated grad night, I was bound for college, and New England's call suited me just fine!

It was a hot July afternoon as my friend, Steve, and I swam over to New Pond's island. I then noticed that we were not the island's only inhabitants. I saw a girl standing on the beach all by herself, gazing out on the lake at a water skier, skimming across the waves. The boat was filled with teens laughing.

I asked Steve, "Who is that girl?"

He answered, "That's Wendy Taylor!"

"People where you live," the little prince said, "grow
five thousand roses in a garden...yet they don't
find what they're looking for...and yet what they're
looking for could be found in a single rose."

—Antoine de Saint-Exupéry, *The Little Prince*

Day Four

God spoke, "Lights! Come out! Shine in Heaven's sky! Separate Day from Night. Mark seasons and days and years. Lights in Heaven's sky to give light to the Earth." And there it was.

God made two big lights, the larger to take charge of Day, the smaller to be in charge of Night, and he made the stars. God placed them in the heavenly sky to light up Earth and oversee Day and Night, to separate light and dark. God saw that it was good. It was evening, it was morning—Day Four.

ANGELS IN DISGUISE

Do not neglect to show hospitality to strangers, for by doing that, some have entertained angels without knowing it.

—Hebrews 13:2 NRSV

It is 6:20 a.m., and from my bedroom window, I can see the outline of the Mingus Mountains in the twilight. The chimes hanging from above my outside bedroom patio seem to be playing a familiar melody. Its identical mate hangs over Wendy's gravesite nine miles away. Whenever I visit, her chimes seem to sing to the ebb and flow of the desert breezes. I know her spirit is smiling!

Wendy was always a sucker for a stranger's hard-luck story. There was an innocence about her that I loved. She had a way of making lifelong friends wherever she went.

When we were first married, every once in a while, we would get knocks on our apartment door in Hollywood from strangers who she just met. Having been raised in Hollywood, I would gently scold her, "You need to have some street sense!" She would always reply, "Don't worry, I know when someone is in need. And when that happens, they are no longer a stranger to me."

Wendy had the soul of an artist and saw beauty in everything she encountered.

Tomorrow is Thanksgiving, and as I lay in my bed, counting my blessings, I give thanks to God for those who have befriended me throughout my life. It seems to me that each person's life is like an unlit candle, ready to flicker in the light of humanity. When ignited, many glow in radiance as they befriend another.

My thoughts turn to those I have never met yet find inspiration from their life stories—as the light from their compassion glimmers in my mind.

It was a cold, damp night on the river's bank when Josef bid goodbye to his comrade Rudolf. The year was 1964. You see, Josef and Rudolf grew up together behind the Iron Curtain, in Bratislava, Czechoslovakia. Now, after all of these years, Josef was going to swim across the Danube and flee to Vienna and freedom, not more than forty kilometers away.

Josef embraced his friend and said in a voice barely louder than a whisper, "When I get to Amereekaa, I will tell the peeple of my oppressed friends here. No matter what happens, I will not forget you, Rudi!"

Rudolf smiled at his friend and quietly said, "*Dekuju*, Josef."

Now in Czech, *dekuju* means "thank you." But in the universal human language of friendship, it could also be said,

> "There are those who pass like ships in the night, who meet for a moment then sail out of sight, with never a backward glance of regret; folks we know briefly then quickly forget. Then there are friends who sail together through quiet waters and stormy weather, helping each other through joy and through strife.

And they are the kind that give meaning
to life" (author unknown).

A little over 150 years ago in Tewksbury, Massachusetts,
a little girl lay hunched up in the fetal position, unrespon-
sive to those around her. You see, so-called "institutions" for
the emotionally ill and physically handicapped were in an
entirely different state of condition in those days.

The disabled were looked upon as only partly human,
neurotics were treated as criminals, and catatonics, those so
withdrawn that they would curl up like sowbugs, well they
would treat those people like animals!

And there was an old charlady who would come into
her room each day to clean the cages. And she had compassion for the little girl. And slowly, ever so slowly, through her
patience and loving touch, she helped to bring that little girl
out of her catatonic state.

Years later, that little girl would go on to help another
little girl by the name of Helen Keller and indirectly helped
to inspire literally millions of deaf, mute, blind, emotionally
ill, physically disabled, and "normal" people!

But you can't help but wonder, what would have happened to Helen Keller if that old charlady hadn't befriended
little Annie Sullivan?

Blind, deaf, and mute, Helen would communicate with
her friend and teacher, Annie, by means of a "touch" sign
language. Amazing!

But in the universal human language of friendship,
many years later, still blind and deaf, Helen would put it
another way. She would write while thinking of her friend
and teacher, Annie:

The best and most beautiful things in this world, cannot be seen or even touched—they must be felt with the heart!

—Helen Keller

The old Japanese man, already well into his eighties, would faithfully meet his retired Mexican friend every day at one o'clock in the park to play some games of checkers.

Although their friendship was barely a year old, they felt as though they knew each other for a lifetime because they both possessed that intangible quality of patience in life to accept each other with dignity, honor, and respect.

It didn't really matter which opponent captured the most checkers to his side of the board, because in the real game, they were playing here; they were on the same side sharing memories of their past.

And when the games were over, and the afternoon grew late, the old Japanese man would rise and then humbly bow and say in his native language, "This time we have spent together means so much to me. Do you understand me?"

And after reading his friend's facial expression, the old Mexican would smile and reply, "No, pienses en eso. El placer fue mio amigo miso!" which means, "Think nothing of it. The pleasure was mine, my friend!"

But in the universal human language of friendship, it could also be said:

I sought my soul, but my soul I could not see. I sought my God. But my God eluded me. I sought my brother, and then I found all three!

—William Blake

James Lowell once said that all God's angels come to us disguised. My patio chimes continue to sway in the breeze with a heavenly ring.

Perhaps there will be angels seated with us tomorrow night as we pause to give thanks!

> An angel stood and met my gaze,
> Through the low doorway of my tent.
> The tent is struck, the vision stays,
> I only know she came and went.

> —James Russell Lowell, *She Came and Went*

A PAUSE IN OUR CADENCE

Whenever you find yourself on the side of the
majority, it is time to pause and reflect.

—Mark Twain

There's a story in the book of Joshua from the Old Testament.
It's about the Battle of Jericho. God instructed Joshua to have
his army march around the city once a day for six days in a
row. While they marched, the soldiers blew their trumpets
as the priests marched with them, carrying the Ark of the
Covenant.

On the seventh day, the Israelites marched around the
city, and at Joshua's command, the army gave a roar, and the
walls came tumbling down.

Our land, our country, our house had a pause in its
cadence last week. The pain of social injustice coupled with
a worldwide pandemic has brought our weary nation to a
halt. It's as though we decided to incarcerate ourselves in our
common place of dwelling.

The sickness in our house has caused a temporary loss
of our national indivisibility. Many protested in anger on the
streets. Maybe it was fate that this dissent time took place
while the "happiest place on earth" was in quarantine.

It triggered memories of when my father's disease compelled our own house to boil pots, pans, and all eating utensils; else we might become infected with his invisible enemy.

But unseen foes come in multiple forms.

Perhaps our national house needed this late spring cleaning just as the property's collective owners clear away the brush, otherwise their home could be completely burned down.

The spark of freedom could ignite the tinder of conscience piled high in the shed of justice. Within that shack is a powder keg. And as the barrel's staves decompose, the vestiges of America's original sin causes the kindling to turn to excelsior.

One can only hope that the cooler heads who pour water into the shed will shout: "Hold on, hold on. Keep your eye on the prize!"

Maybe this time, the real silent majority will join in.

The marches of protest brought back a recollection of me standing in the rain in a crowd on Boston Common. It was five days before my nineteenth birthday in April 1965. I was a freshman attending Suffolk University located just behind the state capitol building and two blocks away from the Common.

I had just finished my last class and started to cut through the Common on my way to catch the train home to Walpole. As I walked through the park in the drizzle, I found myself in a sea of humans.

It had been twenty months since I heard his voice coming from the Lincoln Memorial while traveling on a train bound for New England. This time he was here in person, as his words rang out. He appeared to be a relatively short man in stature standing under a small black umbrella.

But it was the sound of his words that caught my attention. His voice rising in a steady rhythmic cadence: "Now is the time to make brotherhood a reality. *Now. Now* is the time!"

Jesus himself could not have said it better. Now I think of Jesus's message to his disciples and to us in John 13:34–35 NIV:

> I give you a new command: Love each
> other. You must love each other as I have
> loved you. All people will know that you
> are my followers if you love each other.

Fifty-five years have passed since that moment, and the march continues as our nation struggles with making brotherhood a reality.

Yes, there was a skip in the beat of American life that started last week, but hope still remains the pacemaker in our nation's weary heart as we march on!

> This evening, more than ever
> my ancient, despised Hebrew priest
> warped by the hot Arabian sun,
> inflicted his heart-scorching sermon;
> burnishing with impatient feet
> a whisper of duty in my heart,
> commanding, beseeching,
> that I offer on his altar.
> And a strong white-hot wind blew
> my brothers' woes into my veins.
>
> —William Saphier, "Conscience"

A WALL OF A
DIFFERENT COLOR

When the winds of change blow, some people
build walls, and others build windmills.

—Chinese Proverb

If you take the duck boat ride in Boston, you may find one
of those amphibious tour buses to have a Kilroy etched on its
side. While Bernie's inaugural guest photo of him sitting in a
folding chair with flamboyant mittens has gone viral, Kilroy
has been shared in the four corners of the graffiti world since
the start of the second world war.

Kilroy's figure is that of a man who lifts himself up to
the top of a wall. As you look at him from the other side, all
you can see is half of his bald head (sometimes with a few
hairs), two beady eyes, and a long protruding nose hanging
over the wall. Next to his head are two hands gripping the
apex with his stubby fingers hanging on for dear life, under
the characterization are the words *Kilroy was here!*

What is intriguing to me is that whoever reads these
words is reminded that a wall cannot stop anyone who does
not want to be imprisoned from within. During World
War II, American soldiers drew Kilroy wherever they went
throughout the battlefield. There is a story where Adolph

93

Hitler, after seeing Kilroy's image, wondered if Kilroy was some sort of Allied spy seeking to destroy the Third Reich.

Since the dawn of history, walls have been built to keep enemies out and subjects in. It can be argued that the invention of a wall could be one of the most significant inventions in recorded history. Humans have been constructing walls for twelve thousand years.

The most famous of all walls in the world is the Great Wall of China. First completed twenty-three hundred years ago, this wall extends over thirteen thousand miles!

More than one hundred million tons of bricks were used along with earth and rock by peasants and slave labor to construct this, the most immense work of art in mankind's history. The peasants didn't know at the time that they were instruments of an eternal beauty.

It reminds me of how the Pharaoh compelled the Israelites to use straw and mud to construct the walls around the Egyptian cities and palaces. When Moses told Pharaoh to let his people go, he denied them the straw, leaving them with an impossible task. While thousands died in the effort, God's plan was implemented despite the Egyptians.

Then we have the City of David, where Christ was born. Today Bethlehem is surrounded by a wall. Strange that the town foretold to be the birthplace of the one who would free us all is now, to some, under lock and key! The wall is plastered with graffiti. And although tourists can move in and out of Bethlehem with ease, the wall within remains.

Then there are fences—a cheaper way to keep what you hold dear within and invaders out. Here in Arizona, we have barbed wire fences to keep livestock from wandering off while smaller wildlife roam free in and out of the fenced land. It is an affordable way to fence in thousands of acres at a time.

Strange how the foretelling of the one who would set us free of our bonds would don a crown of barbs! But the walls within have no boundary on earth. And some invaders have found a way to penetrate those walls.

The coronavirus known as COVID-19 has wreaked havoc on humanity and caused millions to die so far. Now I am not a microbiologist or immunologist, but I do know that a virus respects no walls, no borders, and has no morality.

This tiny germ needs a host and what better host than the wall of a human blood cell. As I understand it, a virus's genetic material can replicate once attached to the host.

And once the virus has the chance to replicate, it can travel in the bloodstream to a vital organ, usually the lungs. And all those with a weakened immune system could be left defenseless.

On the other hand, most viruses do not invade the human body, and many keep our ecosystems in balance. Some maintain that, without viruses, the larger more complex bacteria could take over the world.

I remember teaching my confirmation class about the parable of the weeds in Matthew 13:24–30 NIV:

> Jesus told them another parable: "The kingdom of heaven is like a man who sowed good seed in his field. But while everyone was sleeping, his enemy came and sowed weeds among the wheat and went away. When the wheat sprouted and formed heads, then the weeds also appeared. The owner's servants came to him and said, "Sir, didn't you sow good seed in your field? Where then did the weeds come from?"

"An enemy did this," he replied. The servants asked him, "Do you want us to go and pull them up?"

"No," he answered, "because while you are pulling the weeds, you may uproot the wheat with them. Let both grow together until the harvest. At that time, I will tell the harvesters: First collect the weeds and tie them in bundles to be burned, then gather the wheat and bring it into my barn."

I had the students do an activity that involved separating larger black beans from smaller grains of white rice with chopsticks. The lesson emphasized that separating evil from good is a monumental task. The class came to the conclusion that we must be careful as we go about life interacting with our fellow man, else we may harm those who are innocent.

Perhaps it is best to do as our Lord commands and just love everyone equally and leave the judgment to God! As for the walls, we build in our lives—all I can say is, *hang in there, Kilroy!*

Life is a solitary cell where walls are mirrors!

—Eugene O'Neill

HOW DO YOU COLOR PAIN?

Even in my sleep, pain which cannot forget falls drop by drop upon my heart until in my own despair, against my will, comes wisdom through the awful grace of God.

—Aeschylus

When I walked into the room, I noticed a little blond-haired boy sitting with the other littles in a circle of colorful miniature chairs. He was staring at the throw rug that seemed only millimeters from his tiny knees.

The pattern on the beige carpet matched the furrowed look on his cherub face. The stare was blank, like the gaze on a marble statue. He clutched at the talking stick as he held it close to his chest. It was adorned with colorful beads and feathers, and when he moved it, it sounded like a rattlesnake.

The other children were holding on to their teddy bears in anticipation. The silence was deafening with ten tiny eyes fixed on him.

The vision brought back memories of our training on how to facilitate grieving children. Then in a short spurt of energy, he shoved the stick to the little girl next to him and murmured, "Pass."

A few years ago, our youth pastor asked our group if we would be willing to start a center for grieving children in the Prescott area. It was one of his lifelong passions.

The people from the New Song Center for Grieving Children in Phoenix were gracious enough to help train us. We followed their model of operation. Our group is called the Heart Song Center for Grieving Children.

Our meetings start with a meal where all the children and their loved ones get to know each other. The groups then meet in one large circle to talk about our theme for the night. Then the adults and children break into their smaller groups. Children are divided by age—littles, five to seven years old; middles, eight to ten years old; and tweens and teens.

Each of the smaller groups has some sort of activity involving the theme for the night—all designed with some type of healing process.

When one is in grief, some say it's like sitting adrift and alone in a rowboat in the middle of the ocean. There you are, without a compass and with the oars laying on the floor.

Grief can be such a personal thing—it robs you of your motivation. You'd like to take the oars and start rowing, but even if you could, where would you go?

As facilitators, our goal is to simply get in their boat and drift with them for a while. We don't even want to touch the oars. In time, with the support of their family, other children in their group, and our love, their ship will begin to have a heading.

We start with a circle of chairs occupied with each child holding a stuffed toy or some object of their affection. In the middle of the ring is a talking stick. It is a symbol of honor, and the one who holds it may speak to the group with whatever feelings they have at the moment.

The talking stick started with the native Americans. It was a carved ornamental staff that became an emblem of authority. In a council meeting, the one who held the talking stick received the utmost respect.

During the night, each group of children would have an activity to do. The activity usually involves something hands-on, to express one's feelings of grief. This particular night, we asked the group to pick a cardboard replica of a key. The child would then draw a picture or write a word that best described what they felt about their loss.

When the activity was over, the group returned to the circle and shared what they drew or wrote. When the talking stick came to the little blond-haired boy, he looked at the others, then looked at the talking stick, and then looked at the key held tightly in his hand.

Then he showed the group what he had drawn. On one side of the key was a smiley face. On the other side was a black tear in the middle of a grey blob. He said remembering his mother makes him smile, and sometimes it makes him very sad.

He told the kids that his key was going into his colorful treasure box at home. He said it was colorful because his treasure box used to hold his colored chalk, and now it contains his happy thoughts and a few of the things he loves.

Then he said, "I keep my treasure box under my bed where no one can see it but me!"

The little blond-haired boy finished the night with a song and a hug as each of the littles bid goodbye to each other for the evening.

Fairies have to be one thing or the other
because being so small they unfortunately have
room for one feeling only at a time.

—J.M. Barrie Peter Pan

CHRISTMAS CARDS IN JULY

With freedom, books, flowers, and the
moon, who could not be happy?

—Oscar Wilde

A little boy, in a cub scout uniform, peddles by my house this morning. His bike, adorned with old glory, tethered to his rear fender flapping in the wind. I notice a glee's look on his face while he does a mini wheelie as he glides by on his bike.

I can only surmise that it is the coming events of the day that gives him such joy. Perhaps he is rehearsing for his part in the parade.

Yes, today is the Fourth of July!

Our town's parade will commence in a couple of hours. It will be followed by a carnival in our park, followed by a spectacular firework display at twilight.

My little cub scout friend reminds me of when I was his age enjoying the summer's freedom. My friends and I were always looking for ways to acquire spending money. Of course, while they had their paper routes, I took a different tack.

My goal was to make a boy's fortune by selling boxes containing an assortment of Christmas cards door-to-door.

After all, my friends got paid two cents for each paper they delivered while I would take in a whole fifty cents for every box of cards I sold!

After dreaming of how I would spend my newfound riches, I quickly discovered that persuading my neighbors to buy Christmas cards in July was not as easy as I thought!

It was a job short-lived!

After that going to the public swimming pool in the morning and selling cold lemonade on hot summer afternoons seemed a lot more satisfying.

Vacations, holidays, and festivals have been part of our world history ever since man realized the unwavering changing of the seasons.

In Kyoto, Japan, the Gion Festival takes place in July and celebrates the purification of disease causing entities with decorated twelve-ton floats. In Rio de Janeiro, carnival is celebrated by millions to bring on the forty days of Lent. And in India, Diwali is a festival of lights celebrated by Hindus, Buddhists, and Sikhs marking the spiritual victory of light over darkness, good over evil, and knowledge over ignorance.

Christmas in July—perhaps the two holidays are, in some strange way, linked in the chain of observance.

I mean, the birth of our nation is a holiday celebrated with sights and sounds followed by a crescendo of colors ending with a bang. And then we have the birth of our Lord. A holiday celebrated with sights and sounds, followed by a crescendo of colors ending with curtains torn, stones rolled away, and a display of light that can never go out!

There is a cactus that grows here in the nearby Sonoran Desert. It is called the *Agave ocahui*. It is known as the Century Plant because people believe it only blooms every hundred years. Truth be told, it really lives for about thirty years. When it is about to die, it puts on a display of beauty and color worth of a cameo in Disney's Fantasia.

What is astounding to me is that our Lord walked the earth for a little over thirty years. And when he was about to die, he put on a display of love for all humanity to follow. And the glow of this love continues to illuminate every corner of our darkened world.

As this Arizona town ends its day with a sky dotted in shades of red, white, and blue and a park full of oohs and aahs, I chuckle to myself as I make my solemn resolution: If a little boy comes knocking on my door, selling a box containing a variety of cards honoring the American Experiment, the birth of our Lord, or all of God's holidays great and small, he would have his first sale hands down!

> Be ashamed to die until you have won
> some victory for humanity.

—Horace Mann

THE GREATEST
SPECTACLE IN RACING

And Elisha prayed, "Open his eyes, Lord, so that
he may see." Then the Lord opened the servant's
eyes, and he looked and saw the hills full of
horses and chariots of fire all around Elisha.

—2 Kings 6:17 NIV

As the Arizona sun goes down the shadows of the rocks
and cactus grow longer as they point toward the Mingus
Mountains. In the foreground, I see a herd of pronghorn take
off over the plain. I call out to them, "Why the hurry?"

One thing is for sure, no need for them to fret. Whatever
predator was causing them to bolt, he or she can't catch them
now.

Did you know that the pronghorn is the fastest group
of land creatures in the western hemisphere? Reaching top
speeds of over sixty miles per hour, these animals have a grace
about them as they sail through the prairie.

Why is it that we humans long to have that same grace
about us as we race through life? Perhaps we have a little bit
of the "tortoise and the hare" etched in our DNA. I think the
longing comes to us when the drive of ambition collides with
the pit stop of patience and reflection.

I suppose all children come into this world with an innate ability to run. I was convinced of this principle as I watched my grandchildren learn to crawl and stand and walk.

And just like their fellow toddlers, once they take their first steps, walking turns to running in no time at all. And once a child can run—they discover they can race!

Ever notice that all children seem to have smiles on their faces when they are running? I think there must be some nerve that extends from toe to tooth. And it triggers the facial features of elation when their little legs shift into fifth gear!

The contest of racing started eons ago. Homer records that chariot racing started in Greece as far back as 800 BC. The Romans advanced the sport to a main event in the Circus Maximus in the sixth century BC.

However I would assume that our modern-day version of this ancient race appears to us each year on or around Memorial Day in Indianapolis. I got the firsthand experience of this race a couple of years ago when I took my planes, trains, and automobile trip.

When I took my seat, I heard the announcer declare, "Ladies and gentlemen, start your engines!"

I never understood what that phrase meant.

I mean, shouldn't all of these high-performance works of art be warmed up and humming beforehand? I guess tradition takes precedence over practicality.

The sound of all these engines firing up is akin to the massed pipers joining in to play "Amazing Grace." While Indy is not the highlands, it's just a stone's throw away from the "Gathering of the Clans" and "Let the Games Begin."

The very first car that I owned was a Triumph TR-10. Although it had an electric starter, it came with a hand crank! I remember using this option, in my college days during a few Boston snowstorms.

Perhaps an Indy 500 pit crew must remember rule number one: Start your engine. Otherwise the tortoise driving that little clunker might just come out ahead of you!

As we travel down life's highway, sometimes we walk, and then we run, and then we sprint, and then we limp along until we have finished the journey.

The apostle Paul wrote to his disciple, Timothy, from his prison cell in Rome while waiting to be executed.

In 2 Timothy 4:6–8 NIV, he said:

> For I am already being poured out like a drink offering, and the time for my departure is near. I have fought the good fight, I have finished the race, I have kept the faith. Now there is in store for me the crown of righteousness, which the Lord, the righteous Judge, will award me on that day—and not only to me but also to all who have longed for his appearing.

No matter how great the spectacle or how loud the pomp and circumstance, every worthy race has a chariot of fire in it.

So be it the push of a button, the turn of a key, or the old college try with a hand crank, ladies and gentlemen, start your engines!

> It does not matter how slowly you go
> as long as you do not stop.
>
> —Confucius

AN ASPEN'S CONCERTO

In three words. I can sum up everything
I've learned about life: It goes on.

—Robert Frost

Aspen trees have always intrigued me. I think it's because of how their leaves blow in the wind. The tree is aptly named the *quaking aspen*. After all, fish swim, birds fly, dogs bark, and aspens quake.

There is a tree that grows out of the granite side of a mountain in the High Sierras. I used to climb by it every time I hiked up to the high country in October.

Suspended twelve feet above the trail, it shoots out about six feet in diagonal fashion as I pass under it. Every time I walked by, it would greet me with its golden leaves aflutter.

The first time I noticed this little guy was about forty years ago. At the time, I said to myself, "This puny sapling will never become a real aspen tree." After all, (1) it is growing out of a rock; (2) it will never survive the sixty-plus-mile-per-hour wind gusts screaming up the mountain walls; and (3) it will never live through the cold, wicked snowstorms of winter at eleven thousand feet and buried under snow and ice for several months of the year!

That was four decades ago. And if I were a betting man, forty years from now, I would wager that it will still be alive and shaking in the wind while its leaves play its concerto to life.

As I sit in front of my fireplace, six hundred miles to the south, I muse over how this little guy got there. Perhaps a leaf from a tree, five thousand feet below the mountain, was enticed into the air currents. Maybe it flew up the canyon walls to finally be deposited in this most unusual domicile.

Or could it be that some bird picked up a twig destined to become a nest only to fall from its grip and then carried in a violent updraft to land in this granite fissure?

Is there randomness in Mother Nature's sphere of existence or a plan in God's circle of life? I personally think our Lord is a very patient God. After all, it must have taken tens of millions of years for that granite to split and become my little friend's nest.

Aspens are a fantastic part of our world. Native Americans found ways to use them for medicinal purposes. They made a tea from the leaves to relieve pain and found ways to heal wounds by making a salve from its buds. They even made a type of bread using the yeast-like powder from its bark.

In 650 BC, the prophet Jeremiah cried out to soothe his pain by asking God, "Is there no balm in Gilead? Is there no physician there?" That balm supposedly came from a poplar tree, a cousin of the quaking aspen.

Yes, aspens have been doctoring people for thousands of years. This incredible tree can live in the harshest of conditions. They can repopulate after a forest fire has destroyed everything in its wake.

Aspen groves can connect their roots with others to become one organism. The oldest known living clone, the

Pando aspen grove in Utah, is eighty thousand years old. It is also one of the largest living organisms on earth. Our satellites have even photographed its massive shape from space.

Can you imagine an alien ship approaching earth to discover that life on this planet exists in this strange living form, trembling with life? I can hear these space travelers chatting with each other, commenting about their first sighting of earth life as they approach our world, "Wow, they really grow them big on the tiny blue planet!"

However, my little friend is not connected to a grove or clone of many. It can't be detected from outer space. It sits there, greeting those who pass by, crooning with its ode to life while anchored in its rock.

Perhaps the sanctity of life can be summed up in this little sprout of beauty, pointing to the heavens and singing in the wind!

Humankind has not woven the web of life. We are but one thread within it. Whatever we do to the web, we do to ourselves. All things are bound together. All things connect.

—Chief Seattle

Day Five

God spoke, "Swarm Ocean with fish and all sea life! Birds fly through the sky over Earth!" God created the huge whales, all the swarm of life in the waters, and every kind and species of flying birds. God saw that it was good. God blessed them: "Prosper! Reproduce! Fill Ocean! Birds, reproduce on Earth!" It was evening, it was morning—Day Five.

SLOW ME DOWN, LORD

Peace is the evening star of the sky, as virtue is
its sun, and the two are never far apart.

—Charles Caleb Colton

Let me begin by wishing you in Hebrew, *Shalom aleichem*,
or in Arabic, *As-salamu alaykum*. Both mean "Peace be upon
you, my friend!" However, peace can sometimes be elusive in
our fast-paced world.

Did you know, as we go through our lives, in warp
speed, Mother Earth is spinning like a top at one thousand
miles per hour while suspended in space? That means, in one
day, we will travel twenty-four thousand miles in one mud-
dled circle.

Or to put it another way, we are traveling at sixty-seven
thousand miles per hour as we revolve around the sun. That
equates to 1.6 million miles in one day! In the time it took
to drink your morning coffee, you have already traveled over
eleven thousand miles on our solar carousel.

And as we spin collectively, our moments of peace
on earth, at times, have been like a mirage bubbling up on
that human highway of life. Détente makes its appearance.
Hostilities crop up in one corner of the world while cease-
fires commence in another region with a pen's stroke.

But armistices are short-lived, and the paper overcoat that cloaks, our shared peace so often dissolves as the raindrops of discord begin to fall. Perhaps, in the end, true peace lives with the individual—that peacemaker who turns the other cheek and dares to let his enemy save face.

We seem to give some trivial pursuit priority of the day, as the sun rises, only to miss those God-given moments of serenity when the sun retires into the night.

Scientists say that you would have taken about 680 million breaths in your life if you live to be eighty years old. That amounts to 8 1/2 million breaths per year. But the thing is, it is what we create between those breaths that matter—those breathtaking moments that define our life.

Maybe the moments we value should not be spent in a focused-driven burst of ambition but rather be moving in harmony with the real purpose of our lives on earth.

As we rush through the day in our labored tasks, engaged in conversation, or behind the wheel of our car, we are fixated on accomplishment and recognition. And as we do so, moments of peace vanish in the wind as we exhale.

There are so many paths to walk on in our chosen lives. And most of them seem to lead away from contentment. The one course that matters most is the one that keeps you focused on a discovery in the beauty of the moment, like when you slow down to notice how the leaves rustle away from you as you walk down a path or to watch a spider build its geometric work of art in anticipation of the night or to gaze at the sky's overture of hues at day's end.

All are containing a tranquil dose of peace within while the earth makes one more revolution!

In the gospel of John, Jesus, the Prince of peace, not only tells His disciples to keep hope in their hearts, but He promises them a peace that passes all understanding.

In John 14:27 NIV, he says:

> Peace I leave you; my peace I give you. I
> do not give to you as the world gives. Do
> not let your hearts be troubled, and do
> not be afraid.

That was over two thousand years ago. And while on the outside, peace is still more challenging to catch than that golden snitch. Jesus's promise remains golden on the inside.

Do you want peace? Just dismount from your stationary horse, step off the carousel, tune out the calliope, and pray the Lord's Prayer. Most people pray it in about thirty seconds, traveling about eight and a half miles as we rotate in place or 560 miles as we pirouette around the sun.

Shalom!

> Nowhere can man find a quieter and more
> untroubled retreat than his own soul.

> —Marcus Aurelius

AN OUTBREAK
OF KINDNESS

Three things in human life are important: The first is to be kind; the second is to be kind; and the third is to be kind.

—Henry James

I love to fly fish. A good fly fisherman is always on the look for some enticing pool of water where a trout might be lurking in the depth near the river's edge. And one of the best conditions where a trout might be searching for its morning meal would be in a little pool with an eddy churning above it.

An eddy is a fascinating phenomenon. In the science of fluid dynamics, it is the swirling of a fluid and the reverse current when the fluid is in a turbulent flow regime.

This particular morning on Oak Creek, a little mayfly floats on top of an eddy. This little guy, like any other mayfly, has a life span of just two days. You might say that he even has the soul of a surfer as he rides the crest of a ripple, jubilant in knowing that he is moving in the opposite direction of the great stream of his world. And as he presents himself to the fish below, his kindness goes unnoticed.

Kindness, mercy, and compassion are such unique and beautiful qualities for us humans. I think in the rankings of human virtue, all three are at the top.

Compassion is probably the greatest virtue in religious tradition. It is the feeling that arises when confronted with another's suffering, and you feel motivated to relieve that suffering.

Kindness comes in the act of unselfishness, self-sacrifice, and consideration for another. This virtue also has a ripple effect when one random act continues for another to pass on to another. It becomes infectious!

Mercy is kindness and compassion given by someone who has the power to provide to another.

Here we are in the middle of a worldwide pandemic where millions are suffering, and there are those whose compassion and kindness kick in and show the real qualities of their humanness. I can only hope that those who have the power to provide mercy do so with dispatch.

Perhaps we come into this world with a kindness gene in our DNA. Maybe it was passed on eons ago when the first of our ancestors extended his hand to help another fallen companion.

I suppose we humans have forever mused, "Is there a heaven? And if there is a heaven, what is heaven like? And more importantly, what do I have to do to get into heaven?"

Perhaps the keys to the gates of heaven are cast with a die. And these dies come in the shapes of kindness, mercy, and compassion. And each key is duplicated with every random act of love committed.

Jesus told us just how important doing a kind act can be. He answered a question posed by a lawyer, and the world was astonished. Like any good lawyer, he would never ask a question that he did not already know the answer. This man was a scribe, meticulous in detail, and lawful correctness.

So he sets out to test Jesus with his question in Luke's gospel as recorded in Luke 10:25–37 NKJV:

> "Teacher, what shall I do to inherit eternal life?"
>
> He said to him, "What is written in the law? What is your reading of it?" So he answered and said, "You shall love the Lord your god with all your heart, with all your soul, with all your strength, and with all your mind,' and 'your neighbor as yourself."
>
> And He said to him, "You have answered rightly; do this and you will live."
>
> But he, wanting to justify himself, said to Jesus, "And who is my neighbor?"
>
> Then Jesus answered and said, "A certain man went down from Jerusalem to Jericho and fell among thieves, who stripped him of his clothing, wounded him, and departed, leaving him half dead.
>
> "Now by chance a certain priest came down that road. And, when he saw him, he passed by on the other side. Likewise, a Levite, when he arrived at the place, came and looked and passed by on the other side. But a certain Samaritan, as he journeyed, came where he was. And, when he saw him, he had compassion. So he went to him and bandaged his

wounds, pouring on oil and wine; and he set him on his own animal, brought him to an inn, and took care of him. On the next day, when he departed, he took out two denarii, gave them to the innkeeper, and said to him, 'Take care of him; and whatever more you spend, when I come again, I will repay you.' So which of these three do you think was neighbor to him who fell among the thieves?"

And he said, "He who showed mercy on him."

Then Jesus said to him, "Go and do likewise."

Our Lord always finds a way to use the least of us to do great things. And the radiance from those who do the tiniest acts of kindness comes from a light source tethered to the one sitting to the right side of His throne.

I could never find the exact dry fly to match the beauty of that little mayfly floating on top of that eddy that morning. *It was a beautiful day!*

That best portion of a good man's life, his little, nameless, unremembered acts of kindness and of love.

—William Wordsworth, *Lyrical Ballads*

IN THE TWINKLING
OF AN EYE

Life can only be understood backwards,
but it must be lived forwards.

—Soren Kierkegaard

My little granddaughter, Wendy, loves to play with her dolls. She dresses them in proper attire as she celebrates, with each in attendance at her three o'clock tea parties. At five years old, I do believe she has developed an eye for fashion.

Whenever we take our afternoon walks, we need to take three bottles of water, one for Wendy, one for Papa, and one for the rocks! As we stroll along by the prairie, we pass by a vast array of high desert rocks. Some are jagged, some volcanic in nature, while others are smooth and round with elliptical oblong shapes.

All of them have one thing in common—*they thirst!*

Little Wendy brought her magnifying glass, and after examining a flowering pear tree leaf, who then came along for the ride, we looked at several rocks up close and personal.

As we walked along, we saw many smooth rounded stones sanded down by what ancient river? The area is rich in dried up tributaries from monsoonal flash floods. We are not far from Bradshaw Mountain, which provides an old profile of an extinct volcano.

When we pour water over the stones, they blossom with a whole spectrum of changing colors. Charcoal-colored rocks turn indigo while gray ones turn opal green—pale-yellow-colored stones become mustard. And sand-colored ones change to bright gold. We saw several two-toned rocks that appeared as if an artist drew the line at its equator. It transformed to half purplish and half mauve.

I think of how important stones have been in world history. As I look at the ruins of the ancient towns in Galilee, I see that all that is left are stone foundations. There has always been very little timber in the Middle East. It seems to me that it was a loose translation of Jesus being a carpenter. Perhaps, he was really a stone mason.

Little Wendy asks me if the rocks are like butterflies who change colors in their cocoons. Another of Wendy's questions go unanswered for the moment, more questions about rocks—questions that segue to more questions, queries that Papa has no immediate answers.

The only plausible comment I can make is to have a little patience. The answers will come like the patience of the rocks—yes, the patience of the rocks. To these stones, we are but a blip in time. The apostle Peter wrote in 2 Peter 3:8 NIV:

> But do not forget this one thing, dear friends: With the Lord, a day is like a thousand years, and a thousand years are like one day.

As we continued down our path, my mind then remembered what Paul wrote to the Corinthians. In 1 Corinthians 15:52 ESV, he wrote:

> In a moment, in the twinkling of an eye, at the last trumpet, for the trumpet will sound, and the dead will be raised imperishable, and we shall be changed.

Perhaps the rocks' patience will someday reveal their answers, but for now, they provide us with their afternoon fashion show.

It's time for my granddaughter to get back home and attend to her dolls, with bedtime stories of our adventure among the stones—stones that put on their show, complete with rocks dressed in full regalia of colors.

Of all the trails in life, the best one is the path adorned with rocks and lizards and birds and desert flowers, including a certain little brown-eyed sunflower stepping among the stones with a bottle of water and a magnifying glass!

> It is the time you have wasted for your rose that makes your rose so important.

> —Antoine de Saint-Exupéry, *The Little Prince*

DESERT WATER BAGS

My soul thirsts for God, for the living God. When
shall I come and behold the face of God?

—Psalm 42:2 NRSV

When I was a child, I remember making the trip by auto
through Death Valley. It was a rough trip back then because
our car didn't have any air conditioning.

My sister and I would sit in the back of our parent's
Henry J looking out the rearview window as we rode along. I
remember seeing a mirage on the highway for the first time.
The water image looked so inviting, especially in a place
called *Death Valley*.

Our car, like most others, had a canvas desert water bag
hanging from the front bumper. I could never get over how
the water within that canvas bag stayed so cool while suspended a mere six inches from the blacktop of a highway,
radiating to a surface temperature of more than 160 degrees.

Whenever we stopped, I would run to the water bag
and take a gulp as though it was my last. No matter how hot
it was on the outside, the water on the inside seemed cold
and refreshing, just as if it came out of the fridge.

My senses were fooled. Mirages and desert water bags
have a way of doing that.

A little cool water can always take the heat away. It just goes to show that water will always beat fire if there's enough of it.

Astronomers and geologists will tell you that about 4.5 billion years ago, our solar system came into existence with a big bang, lots of fire, a newborn star with revolving planets, and our earth oozing molten lava.

Yes, there was fire, fire everywhere!

But as God created the firmament, our planet cooled down, and life began to flourish. While water is essential to life, it cannot nourish the spirit. Only living water can quench a parched soul.

I can imagine how Ezekiel felt when the spirit of the Lord placed him in the midst of a valley of death. The Babylonians had attacked Israel, and Ezekiel's vision showed a vanquished valley floor full of the defeated bleached bones.

If you walk through Death Valley today, you might come across a shell, the last remnant of some living crustaceans who once enjoyed the ancient cool waters of a vibrant sea some 1.7 billion years ago.

If you gaze out on the horizon, you might assume that this valley of bones and shells is lifeless and barren. But if one looks closer, life is teaming with our Lord's creatures. They are the ancestors of bones and shells that have come to life to dwell in an ecosystem touched by the cooling hand of God.

Two thousand six hundred years ago, the Lord spoke to the prophet Ezekiel and gave him instructions through a vision. In Ezekiel 37:1–14, it says:

> The hand of the Lord was on me, and he brought me out by the spirit of the Lord and set me in the middle of the valley; it was full of bones. He led me back

and forth among them, and I saw a great many bones on the floor of the valley, bones that were very dry. He asked me, "Son of man, can these bones live?"

I said, 'Sovereign Lord, you alone know."

Then he said to me, "Prophesy to these bones and say to them, 'Dry bones, hear the word of the Lord! This is what the Sovereign Lord says to these bones: I will make breath enter you, and you will come to life. I will attach tendons to you and make flesh come upon you and cover you with skin. I will put breath in you, and you will come to life. Then you will know that I am the Lord.'"

So I prophesied as I was commanded. And as I was prophesying, there was a noise, a rattling sound, and the bones came together, bone to bone. I looked, and tendons and flesh appeared on them, and skin covered them. But there was no breath in them.

Then he said to me, "Prophesy to the breath. Prophesy, son of man, and say to it, This is what the Sovereign Lord says: Come, breath from the four winds, and breathe into these slain that they may live.'" So I prophesied as He commanded me, and breath entered them. They came to life and stood up on their feet—a vast army.

Then He said to me, "Son of man, these
bones are the people of Israel. They say,
'Our bones are dried up, and our hope is
gone. We are cut off.'"

Therefore prophesy and say to them:
"This is what the Sovereign Lord says:
My people, I am going to open your
graves and bring you up from them. I
will bring you back to the land of Israel.
Then you, my people, will know that I
am the Lord, when I open your graves
and bring you up from them. I will put
My spirit in you, and you will live, and
I will settle you in your own land. Then
you will know that I, the Lord, have spoken, and I have done,' declares the Lord."

Next time when you are walking in a desert of hopelessness and see no way out, be thankful for the cooling touch
from the hand of our Lord.

Even in the driest of places, when you think all is lost
and life is gone, our Lord gives us renewal and hope with the
most mundane of things.

Yes, mirages and desert water bags have a way of doing
that!

But those who drink the water that I will
give them will never be thirsty again.

—John 4:14 NRSV

MOVERS AND SHAKERS

All mankind is divided into three classes: those that are immovable, those that are movable, and those that move.

—Benjamin Franklin

In his hilarious comedy routine, George Carlin argues that the meaning to life is trying to find a place to keep your stuff. He said, "If you didn't have so much stuff, you wouldn't need a house." He goes on, "That's all your house is, it's a place to keep your stuff while you go out and get more stuff." He then surmises that a house is just a pile of stuff with a lid on it!

And when your stuff becomes more than your house can hold, what do you do?

"Gotta get a bigger house!"

Little did I know that this one gluttonous American dilemma would be tied to my future when I was in high school.

I'm sure movers have been around since the first caveman strapped whatever stuff he had on his back and ventured out of his cave, looking for another place to call home.

When Adam and Eve had to pack up and leave Eden, there probably wasn't too much argument over what to take. They didn't have that much stuff to carry—maybe an extra fig leaf!

I began working part-time as a mover and packer. The job even paid for a significant portion of my college education. For the next forty-five years, I would sell, supervise, train, manage, and own a moving company—an industry all predicated on the notion of moving and watching over people's stuff.

I figure my involvement with more than sixty thousand relocations in that near half century has given me one conclusion: *Moves are like snowflakes, each one is unique.*

Many customers had fame like Bob Hope, Desi Arnaz, and Mohammad Ali. Other shipments included historical artifacts, while others included rocket propulsion equipment for NASA. Some involved moving corporations with hundreds of employees over a weekend.

Many carried their station in life, like corporate executives and military generals. But most were average, everyday run-of-the-mill families looking for a new start.

Every relocation includes one common thread—*stress.* Did you know that moving is one of the most stressful events that can happen in your life? It ranks right up there with the death of a loved one, a life-threatening disease, divorce, financial ruin, and then comes moving!

Stress and stuff make strange bedfellows. I say you've gotta trust your mover as much as you would trust your doctor or banker. After all, who else would you let take all your worldly possessions, load it into a box on wheels, and drive off, sometimes thousands of miles, expecting to see it again safe and unharmed?

Moving can be an art and can be a science. Most of all, moving provides an opportunity to have a little empathy for the one in a state of transition.

Did you know that the average book carton can hold up to sixty pounds of books and papers? But that is minuscule compared to the volume of memories contained in one little thought. And these recollections crop up in abundance when you are preparing to move on in your life.

One of my most special moves was back when I was still in college, working as a helper. It was New Year's Eve day.

Our two-person crew was called in the late afternoon to reposition a few pieces of furniture for this little old lady within her apartment. After twenty minutes of moving, she asked us to sit with her in the living room and chat. And for the next three and a half hours, she did the talking while paying our hourly rate.

Jesus had something to say about movers and shakers. The disciples became movers and shakers the minute Jesus spoke to them in Mark's gospel. Mark 6:7–13 NIV records:

> Calling the twelve to Him, he began to send them out two by two and gave them authority over impure spirits.
>
> These were his instructions: "Take nothing for the journey except a staff—no bread, no bag, no money in your belts. Wear sandals but not an extra shirt. Whenever you enter a house, stay there until you leave town. And if any place will not welcome you or listen to you, leave that place and shake the dust off your feet as a testimony against them."
>
> They went out and preached that people should repent. They drove out many demons and anointed many sick people with oil and healed them.

As the waning hours of the year came to an end, the little old lady shared memories of her life with two strangers sipping her coffee.

My celebration of New Year's Eve with Wendy was a few hours late that night, but I learned two truths as that last day of the year ended. First is that every person on earth has a story to tell. And second is that the one who listens to their story becomes more richer for it.

And we'll take a cup of kindness yet for auld lang syne!

There are things that we never want to let go of, people we never want to leave behind. But keep in mind that letting go isn't the end of the world. It's the beginning of a new life.

—Unknown

PRAYERS OF STEEL

Lay me on an anvil, O God.
Beat me and hammer me into a crowbar.
Let me pry loose old walls.
Let me lift and loosen old foundations.

Lay me on an anvil, O God.
Beat me and hammer me into a steel spike.
Drive me into the girders that hold a skyscraper together.
Take red-hot rivets and fasten me into the central girders.
Let me be the great nail holding a skyscraper through blue
nights into white stars.

—Carl Sandburg, Prayers of Steel

When Saint Francis prayed his famous prayer, he reminded us that a true Christian's mark is forged within us when we become an instrument for God. Saint Francis was asking God to live the life that He would have us live. And in doing so, sometimes the process can be painful.

Whenever I visited Maine in my business travels, I would always schedule a stay at Boothbay Harbor. I loved to take a casual stroll at day's end with the view of the harbor. It always gave me a sense of peace watching the fishing boats moored in the bay and safe for the night. Maybe moorings and people have a lot in common.

Some people are like moorings, battered by the waves and sitting too close to the rocky shore, yet they remain anchored in place. And when they know that a hurricane is approaching, they endure and continue to take the brunt of the waves, knowing their true purpose in life.

The mooring connects the anchor to the sea's floor, allowing all to hold on and be safe even with an approaching storm. As for the mooring, it's left with no choice but to pray—prayers that cry out for those who are lost, for those who have become separated from the crowd.

I suppose humans in every corner of the world utter some sort of prayer for a mooring to appear when looking for safe harbor—one soul who welcomes another soul into their sanctuary after drifting on their sea of desolation.

One particular prayer must have had its seed in the mind of a shepherd boy as he lay on his fleece on a cold starry night in the Judean desert, looking up at the Milky Way. His name was David.

In Psalm 19 NKJV, he writes,

> The heavens declare the glory of God;
> And the firmament show His handiwork.
> Day unto day utters speech,
> And night unto night reveals knowledge.
> There is no speech nor language
> Where their voice is not heard.
> Their line has gone out through all the
> earth,
> And their words to the end of the world.

Some say that prayers are simply a conversation with God and conversations that go back to when Adam and Eve fled the garden after a brief chat with a particular serpent.

Shortly after that, God questions their son Cain as to his brother Abel's whereabouts. And Cain's response is in the form of another question.

"Am I my brother's keeper?"

In Genesis 6, God speaks to Noah by giving him specific instructions on surviving a catastrophe by building a vessel. In my mind's eye, I can picture Noah in Marine's uniform, saluting and thinking, *It's time to do or die!*

The Dead Sea Scrolls confirmed there was a man named Melchizedek. The fourteenth chapter of Genesis mentions him. One would have to assume that he was the very first high priest of the temple.

He burned incense with the belief that, as he prayed and as the aroma of the smoke ascended, it was pleasing to God. To this day, the burning of incense in religious ceremonies mark the occasion as holy and special.

One needs to be careful when having a conversation with the Almighty. Job found out. Here was a man who lost everything—his home, children, servants, and livestock.

So Job becomes angry and laments in Job 7:4–6, 11 NRSV:

> When I lie down, I say, "When shall I rise?
> But the night is long.
> And I am full of tossing until dawn.
> My flesh is clothed with worms and dirt;
> my skin hardens then breaks out again.
> My days are swifter than a weaver's shuttle,
> And come to their end without hope.
> Therefore I will not restrain my mouth;
> I will speak in the anguish of my spirit"

I will complain in the bitterness of my
soul.

Of course the Lord listened to him just like He listens
to each of us who babbles. And like most parents, after hearing our children's rant, He tells us to stop talking and listen.

Then God finally answers Job in a whirlwind in Job
38:2–7 NRSV:

> Who is this that darkens counsel by
> words without knowledge?
> Gird up your loins like a man,
> I will question you, and you shall declare
> to me.
> Where were you when I laid the founda-
> tion of the earth?
> Tell me, if you have understanding.
> Who determined its measurements—
> surely you know!
> Or who stretched the line upon it?
> On what were its bases sunk,
> or who laid its cornerstone?
> when the morning stars sang together
> and all the heavenly beings shouted for
> joy?

And after that admonition, whether Job faced east,
west, north, or south—he was not at peace.

As the Native Americans smoke their pipes, history tells
us that they prayed for peace while the smoke carried up to
the four directions.

I suppose that prayers and conversations with God
always end up on a path to righteousness. Perhaps God

allows you to become an instrument for His work. Maybe you become that nail holding up a high-rise. And if you are a skyscraper, you might have the uncanny ability to see how others become instruments for God's handiwork!

> Lord, make me an instrument of thy peace.
> Where there is hatred, let me sow love,
> Where there is injury, pardon;
> Where there is doubt, faith;
> Where there is despair, hope;
> Where there is darkness, light;
> And where there is sadness, joy.

> O Divine Master, grant that I may not so
> much seek
> to be consoled as to console,
> to be understood as to understand,
> to be loved, as to love.

> For it is in giving that we receive,
> It is in pardoning that we are pardoned,
> and it is in dying that we are born to
> eternal life.

—St. Francis of Assisi

CAMOUFLAGED

Nature always wears the colors of the spirit.

—Ralph Waldo Emerson

My spot on the prairie is so quiet this morning.

Sunrise has come and gone. It is as if I were in a scene from some silent movie only everything is still. The only motion I see is the passing of a cream-colored cloud creeping across the stratosphere. I'm entertained as I watch this cotton candy image transform from a cone shape with a cowlick to a cylindrical blob and then vanish.

I can feel the rhythm of my heartbeat as I look out over the horizon and see the white caps of the San Francisco Peaks 125 miles away. The only thing that tells me I am in the scene is the crispness of the air as I breathe in. The warmth of my coffee cup is soothing.

As I focus on the scenery, I look down at what appears to be a combination of terracotta sandstone, gravel, and twigs—it starts to move.

Now I see. It's looking at me!

He cocks his head for a few seconds to size up this massive form sitting in a camp chair—friend or foe? The canyon spotted whiptail lizard then scurries behind an ocotillo.

Now that the sun is up perhaps, he is looking to get a little warmth from the chill of dawn.

It is so amazing how each of God's desert creatures blends in with the environment. Today, no bird of prey has spotted him from above so this little guy can rest easy. His Plan A has worked well. And even if a predator were to grab his whiptail, the tail would simply dislodge allowing him to escape. The muscles in the separated appendage will continue to contract and keep the predator occupied while the whiptail makes his exit.

Yes, it is always best for this Teiidae creature to have a Plan B.

Of course, Plan Bs should only be used sparingly as it takes a lot of energy to grow another tail, not to mention the loss of his stored food supply.

Neither plan was needed to fool the huge form sitting in the camp chair. The whiptail is diurnal, so it is happy to see the first rays of light. I wonder how many sunrises he has seen from his dwelling? What a great spot to watch from!

Such a contrast to the hustle and bustle of the city with all its deafening sounds of humanity.

But in a way, whiptails and people have something in common—they camouflage themselves. The whiptail's markings and colors allow him to blend in with the landscape, while humans camouflage themselves with their words.

Words have a way of changing another's perception. Some words can be flattering and even patronizing. Other words can be of deceit and deception. Still, others can be of encouragement and compassion.

There used to be a TV program called, "What's My Line."

The contestants tried to keep the panelists from guessing what they did for a living by changing the tone of their voice when answering a question. The panelists could only ask a question that called for a yes or no answer.

In the end, it seemed that the panelists more often than not found out who the contestant was before the time was up.

Maybe it's the words we choose to answer questions asked that provide us with our camouflage. Politicians have refined this dance to an art form.

I think the whiptail and the writer of the Gospel of Mark have something in common. Just as the whiptail sheds his tail the disciple Mark, sheds his tunic to escape his pursuers.

When a crowd sent by the Pharisees armed with swords and clubs came to arrest Jesus in the Garden of Gethsemane, they also tried to grab Mark.

In the Gospel of Mark 14:51–52 NRSV, it says:

> A certain man was following Him, wearing nothing but a linen cloth. They caught hold of him, but he left the linen cloth and ran off naked.

It seemed that Mark lived to preach his message another day just like this little guy hiding behind the ocotillo.

As for the huge form sitting in the camp chair, well he's just happy to have taken in another beautiful sunrise!

Heaven is under our feet as well as over our heads.

—Henry David Thoreau

Day Six

God spoke, "Earth, generate life! Every sort and kind: cattle and reptiles and wild animals—all kinds." And there it was: Wild animals of every kind, cattle of all kinds, every sort of reptile and bug. God saw that it was good.

God spoke, "Let us make human beings in our image, make them reflecting our nature So they can be responsible for the fish in the sea, the birds in the air, the cattle, and yes, Earth itself, and every animal that moves on the face of Earth."

God created human beings; he created them godlike, reflecting God's nature. He created them male and female.

God blessed them. "Prosper! Reproduce! Fill Earth! Take charge! Be responsible for fish in the sea and birds in the air, for every living thing that moves on the face of Earth."

Then God said, "I've given you every sort of seed-bearing plant on Earth and every kind of fruit-bearing tree, given them to you for food. To all animals and all birds, everything that moves and breathes, I give whatever grows out of the ground for food." And there it was.

God looked over everything he had made; it was so good, so very good! It was evening, it was morning—Day Six.

TO BE A PIPER

Music is nothing else but wild sounds
civilized into time and tune.

—Thomas Fuller

What is it about the sound of a bagpipe that suddenly causes my soul to become a wayfaring stranger?—sometimes wandering into a forest of resolve, other times marching in unison with the sound of my ancestors, all the time in lockstep seeking meaning to my life.

I don't know what it is that affects me in such a manner. There is a familiarity to the sound—like my mother's voice calling me to dinner at day's end.

Perhaps it is the sound of human dignity that plays on, sometimes in tribute, occasionally in melancholy, always in love.

I think that there are so many instruments that make up the great symphony orchestra of life. The flute puts the tune to flight; the timpani play in anticipation of some significant announcement. The cello differs from the violin to give deeper, warmer tone, and the trumpet signals the start of yet another battle.

But the bagpipe plays on to set your soul on fire! It is an instrument that beckons your spirit to sail, as Danny Boy's mother proclaimed, "From glen to glen and down the mountainside."

And play on it will! While other woodwinds and brass instruments require the musician's breath to make its music, the bagpipe has a way to continue its tune even when the piper stops to draw in another breath. It has bellows made of goat or sheepskin by which the piper pumps under his arm, allowing the pipe to continue its melody—an instrument that actually plays on after the player ceases to breathe into it!

The consensus of thought is that the bagpipe originated in Egypt circa 400 BC. While there is a widespread belief that Emperor Nero played the fiddle when Rome burned in AD 64, another camp believes he played a form of bagpipe. Historians point out that the fiddle didn't even come into existence until the eleventh-century AD.

The Bible mentions the pipes in the third chapter of the book of Daniel 3:4–7 NIV:

> Then the herald loudly proclaimed, nations and peoples of every language, this is what you are commanded to do; as soon as you hear the sound of the horn, flute, zither, lyre, harp and pipe, you must fall down and worship the image of gold that King Nebuchadnezzar has set up. Whoever does not fall down and worship will immediately be thrown into a blazing furnace.

It seems that King Nebuchadnezzar made an image out of gold and gave a decree throughout all of his kingdom. Everyone who heard the sounds from his grandiose orchestra needed to bow down or be burned to death.

When three respected Jews, Shadrach, Meshach, and Abednego, refused to bow down, King Neb ordered them into the furnace.

When his guards peered into the fire, they saw Shadrach, Meshach, and Abednego, accompanied with a fourth soul, walking among the flames. The fourth appeared to be an image of the son of the gods.

I can't help but wonder that the four were dancing to the tune of the pipes as they rejoiced in the grace of God.

The Scottish journalist, Neil Munro, once said:

> The tales have been recounted that in the Home Isles in the old religion, well before Christianity ever came there, the ancient Celts knew that all the sounds that mankind could make, only the pipes could be heard in both worlds.

Perhaps true pipers dwell on a mountaintop so high they can see the images of humankind—past, present, and future—in the valleys below.

Sometimes, the pipes' call can move one wretched soul to salvation and maybe nudge the earth's axis toward the sounds of the heavenly hosts!

Play on!

> This old barbaric music has magic in it. It transforms the Gael. It reawakens the depths of the being in this century, impressions, moods, feelings inherited from a wild, untamed ancestry for thousands of years and gives them strong wine, that strength of arm, and that endurance of soul, which makes them invincible.

—Michael MacDonagh, *The Irish at the Front* 1916

CHEEK TO CHEEK

Come and, trip it as ye go,
On the light fantastic toe,
And in thy right hand lead with thee,
The mountain-nymph, sweet Liberty:
And if I give thee honor due,
Mirth, admit me to thy crew,
To live with her, and live with thee,
In unreproved pleasures free.

—John Milton, *L'Allegro*

My granddaughter and I were invited to a dance last night. We stepped out in front of our house and watched Jupiter and Saturn trip the light fantastic.

It was *the cotillion of the gods.*

The couple of honor was a sight to behold. Saturn dressed in her hooped gown sequined with comets and asteroids, and Jupiter decked out in his Europa tuxedo and Ganymede cummerbund.

The December night was cold, and the moon was blushing. The lights of the sky hung suspended as if in a trance while they gazed as these two performed their heavenly waltz.

The convergence of these planetary giants occurs about every twenty years. But a galactic cheek to cheek rendezvous like this takes place very sporadically.

The last time they danced this close was almost four centuries ago, in 1623, when Galileo might have looked up at the heavens in awe and saw the moons he discovered twinkling brighter. Perhaps their sparkles were putting on a coming-out party as debutantes often do.

Before that, this stunning couple danced eight hundred years ago, in 1226, when Genghis Khan roamed the land and conquered settlements along the Silk Road. Who knows? Maybe Genghis looked up with pause and shouted, "Where is my ticket to the dance?"

But why are they such strangers in the night and for such long interludes? Well for one thing, these two are separated by almost half a billion miles. And for another, their color, density, and planetary behavior differ. Saturn's parents, Caelus and Terra, might disapprove.

Alas, they are truly worlds apart!

However, when the time is right, and the cosmic makeup sets in, the winds of space beckon, and their gravitational pull is something they cannot fight, it's a love story for the universe!

Of course, this would be a lingering slow dance as the music plays on this, the longest day of the year. It is just seventy-two hours from Christmas morning. Little Wendy is concerned if these events might delay Santa Claus's arrival. She asks if Santa might be looking in. Perhaps his reindeer might be watching, but Santa is way too busy to notice as his worldwide journey is about to commence.

Some in history believed this dance to be the Christmas Star. The German renaissance astronomer Johannes Kepler, theorized that this "Christmas Star," the one that the magi followed in pursuit of the nativity, could have been the dance of Jupiter and Saturn.

There is an account of the Christmas Star as told in the book of Matthew. In Matthew 2:1–12 NIV, it records,

> After Jesus was born in Bethlehem in Judea, during the time of King Herod, magi from the east came to Jerusalem and asked, "Where is the one who has been born king of the Jews? We saw His star when it rose and have come to worship Him."

> When King Herod heard this, he was disturbed and all Jerusalem with him. When he had called together all the people's chief priests and teachers of the law, he asked them where the Messiah was to be born. "In Bethlehem in Judea," they replied, "for this is what the prophet has written:

> "But you, Bethlehem, in the land of Judah, are by no means least among the rulers of Judah; for out of you will come a ruler who will shepherd my people Israel."

> Then Herod called the magi secretly and found out from them the exact time the star has appeared. He sent them to Bethlehem and said, "Go and search carefully for the Child. As soon as you find him, report to me so that I too may go and worship Him."

After they had heard the king, they went on their way, and the star they had seen when it rose went ahead of them until it stopped over the place where the child was. When they saw the star, they were overjoyed. On coming to the house, they saw the child with his mother, Mary, and they bowed down and worshipped him. Then they opened their treasures and presented Him with gifts of gold, frankincense, and myrrh. And having been warned in a dream not to go back to Herod, they returned to their country by another route.

Perhaps it was the dance of Jupiter and Saturn that guided the magi. Either way, the heavens celebrated the birth of the one who would save the world.

I have often wondered what Herod Antipas really thought when he saw Jesus face-to-face. The Jewish historian Flavius Josephus records that Herod Antipas was in his early teens when his father, King Herod the Great, dispatched soldiers to kill all the boys in Bethlehem and its vicinity who were two years old or under.

Could the boy Herod Antipas have seen and heard his father celebrating over killing a would-be Child King? What could he have thought when faced with Jesus of Nazareth thirty plus years later?

Maybe my father didn't get the job done back then?

All the while the Christmas Star was watching as it swayed to the tune of salvation!

As wisps of clouds streak across the western sky, signaling a call for the last dance, Little Wendy asks me when the next spectacular dance will be. I tell her it will be in sixty years, and she will be sixty-five years old.

She asks me if I'll be there. I tell her that her grand-mother and I will be watching from the other side of the pantheon ballroom!

> If Jupiter and Saturn meet,
> What a cop of mummy wheat!
> The sword's a cross, thereon He died:
> On breast of Mars the goddess sighed.

—William Butler Yeats, "Conjunctions"

AS DUST BEFORE
THE WIND

The bells of the Gion monastery in India echo with the warning that all things are impermanent. The blossoms of the sala trees teach us through the hues that what flourished must fade. The proud do not prevail for long but vanish like a spring night's dream. In time the mighty too, succumb; all are dust before the wind.

—The Tale of Heiki, Anonymous

There is a bell that sits in my wife's curio cabinet. It looks so out of place. It's not made of glass or crystal or even porcelain. It has no handle, no inside clapper to give it sound. And it would take quite an effort to break it.

It's made of bronze, and the ringing of this bell reminds me that nothing is permanent. It is a replica of a Buddhist temple bell known as the *bonsho*. These bells are used to summon monks to prayer throughout many Buddhist temples.

Funny how the ringing of a bell can signal some type of significant event in one's life.

The largest bell ever made, the great bell of Dhammazedi, was said to have weighed over 650,000 lbs.

The bell is now supposedly resting on the bottom of the Yangon River in Myanmar after thieves attempted to steal it. What poetic justice!

As if to say, "The sounds within me will never be heard by those who have evil intentions!"

Yes, bells and rivers have always had a connection in history. I think rivers remind us how there is a flow to life, while bells provide life's celebration and meaning.

There is a custom in Japan where a bell is rung 108 times on New Year's Eve. It is a practice called *joya-no-kane. Joya* is a Japanese word for New Year's Eve and *Kane* is Japanese for bell.

Tourists and Buddhist monks enthusiastically ring the bell 108 times just before the dawn of the new year. Buddhist wisdom teaches us that there are 108 human desires that can limit our full human potential. And by the striking of the bell, we can be cleansed of our troubles. The tradition has been around for centuries.

Of course, we in America consider it a solemn honor to take pause and remember those victims of 9/11. Our hearts are in unison as the ringing of a bell is struck 2,983 times paying homage while each soul's name is read.

And whenever a firefighter loses his or her life in the line of duty, the ringing of a fire bell is struck three times in three cycles to honor the brave hero.

Bells have been tolled in every corner of the world since man first experienced his feelings of *pathos* or joy. They give light to what CS Lewis said, "God whispers to us in our pleasures, speaks in our conscience, but shouts to us in our pains. It is His megaphone to rouse a deaf world."

There is a bridge in the state of Washington called the Deception Pass Bridge. The bridge spans over Deception Pass to Whidbey Island in Puget Sound.

Apparently George Vancouver gave it its name because he thought that Whidbey was a peninsula.

I suppose there are many bridges to nowhere that appear in our lives. They are full of promise as we begin to cross over only to find that we may have made a wrong choice.

Then a bell rings in our mind, and we finally make that U-turn that keeps us from going into nothingness.

When the Apostle Paul was addressing the Corinthians about spiritual gifts, he mentions bells in his famous love chapter in the bible. He wrote in 1 Corinthians 13:1–2 NRSV:

> If I speak in the tongues of mortals and of angels, but have not love, I am a noisy gong or a clanging cymbal. And if I have prophetic powers, and understand all mysteries and all knowledge, and if I have all faith, so as to remove mountains, but have no love, I am nothing.

I suppose in the grand scheme of things we are as dust before the wind. And come New Year's Eve, in the tradition of the joya-no-kane, I will give Wendy's bell a go!

> No man is an island, entire in itself.
> Each is a piece of the continent, a part of the main.
> If a clod be washed away by the sea, Europe is the less.
> As well as if promontory were.
> As well as if a manor of thine own or of thine friends were.
> Each man's death diminishes me.

LARRY GORDON

For I am involved in mankind.
Therefore, send not to know for whom
the bell tolls,
It tolls for thee.

—John Donne, *For Whom the Bell Tolls*

CONSIDER THE ANT

Every ant knows the formula of its anthill. Every
bee knows the formula of its beehive. They
know it in their own way, not in our way.

—Fyodor Dostoevsky

As I step out of my front door, I see my little granddaughter
playing on my walkway. She is bent over with her magnifying
glass in hand and focused on the ground.

I could tell she had a bead on some tiny creature with
her glass moving erratically like a slot car racing down the
track from one hairpin turn to another. She said she is watching an ant. She named it Dizzy because it kept zigzagging.

When Hamlet exclaimed, "What a piece of work is
man," his thoughts of humanity were in admiration. After
all, man is noble, the paragon of animals, even like a god.
Then when he looked closer, he thought of man's condition
with despair. He even concluded his reflection by declaring
that we are the quintessence of dust!

I suppose, if man were to look down at the soil, he might
see some examples of improvement. King Solomon thought
so. In Proverbs 6:6–8 NIV, he advises us to consider the ant:

Go to the ant, you sluggard;
consider its ways and be wise!

It has no commander,
no overseer or ruler,
yet it stores its provisions in summer
and gathers its food at harvest.

Ants are amazing creatures that come in all sizes and colors: black, white, red, yellow, even blue and green. And they are numerous.

Someone once said, "If there was a scale large enough to put all the humans in the world on one side and all the ants on the other, the scales would be balanced!"

And they possess so many overlooked virtues.

First, they are survivors. They have continued to thrive for over one hundred and fifty million years.

An ant can survive underwater for more than twenty-four hours. Some wingless tree ants will jump off a high tree, escaping a predator, and glide in the wind using their rear legs as rudders. They can then land on another tree using their legs to secure their landing.

I'd say that the most remarkable survivor of all is the queen ant. This lady can live for up to thirty years, giving birth throughout her entire life span. Her sole purpose in life is to ensure that the colony lives on.

Second, ants are farmers and providers. Here on the Arizona high desert, the red harvester ants will search for vegetation and plant seeds. When they find them, they will carry them back to their nest. Other ants in the colony will chew the seeds and make a dough-like substance. Then they will bring it out in the sun to bake. When done, they bring the cookie-like food back into the nest. They then eat it in the winter. Can you imagine eating Aunt Sassy's cookies on a cold winter day!

Third, they are caretakers and have a symbiotic relationship with the environment. Ever notice when you walk by a line of ants and accidentally kick something on their path, they rush to move the debris out of their way?

Ants are very clean creatures. Whenever two of them meet on the trail, they will disinfect each other in a cleaning gesture, then go on their way.

When a colony of ants finds an acacia tree, they will move in to protect the tree from pests and fungus. The only other insects they will allow in the tree are bees. The bees and the ants then promote the life of the tree.

Fourth, they are fearless protectors. There are army ants that are not afraid to attack something hundreds of times larger than them. Their mission is always to defend their colony and their young whatever the cost.

Even when an army ant's body becomes separated from its head, it will not let go of its bite. Doctors in Africa have learned from the natives that the mandibles of an army ant can be used as sutures for an open wound. So an ant can even heal a human!

Finally, ants will sacrifice themselves for others. Some ants protect their nests from foreign invasion by exploding themselves. They release a toxin that kills the invader and themselves in the process.

During a flood, ants will make a raft as they link up together. The ants on the bottom of the raft sacrifice themselves so that others may live.

We humans can learn a thing or two from the ants when it comes to loving our neighbor.

Just as the Gospel of John 15:12–13 NRSV says:

> This is my commandment, that you love
> one another as I have loved you. No one

has greater love than this, to lay down
one's life for one's friends.

The breeze picks up, and a few leaves rustle across my
front yard. Dizzy has long since escaped the scrutiny of my
granddaughter's monocle. She is now engrossed in the exam-
ination of other tiny specimens.

I think that King Solomon was so right when he advised,
Consider the ant!

All good work is done the way ants do things: little by little!

—Lafcadio Hearn

THE SPIRIT OF MOLOKAI

We must learn to regard people less in the light of what they
do or omit to do and more in the light of what they suffer.

—Dietrich Bonhoeffer

It was another beautiful day in paradise! Before sunrise, I got
up to catch the 6:00 a.m. boat from Lahaina bound for the
Isle of Molokai. My wife and I were celebrating our fiftieth
wedding anniversary at the Ritz Carlton on Maui.

On this particular day, Wendy decided to stay at the
resort, enjoy the food, lounge by the pool, and read her book.
She was not about to board a small craft only to be tossed
to and fro while crossing the Pailolo Channel. This churning body of water is one of the windiest and roughest in the
Hawaiian archipelago.

The Hawaiian word *pai* means "to lift," and the word
oloole means "to shift."

The captain headed our vessel for the western tip of
Molokai only to arrive an hour and a half later near the
island's eastern end. We then hugged the shoreline back up
toward the west, avoiding the pull of the Pailolo current. We
arrived at the halfway point toward the island's western end.

I counted fourteen waterfalls cascading down the cliff
walls as we chugged along. The falls gave off blowing mists of
vapor clouded with the colors of the rainbow.

Molokai is somewhat rectangular, which lends itself to have the longest running white sand beaches and the largest fringing coral reef on earth. It also has the world's highest sea cliffs.

The most prominent geographical feature of the island is the Kalaupapa Peninsula. When I arrived at the top of the peninsula, I was awestruck. As I looked down at the inlet below, I could see the ill-faded town of Kalaupapa.

It was breathtaking to see this village surrounded by the Pacific Ocean stretching out in three directions, only to be imprisoned by a backdrop of sixteen-hundred-foot cliffs. The vision reminded me of peering over Niagara Falls. I felt a sense of pull where the sound, the mist, and the sheer perception of magnificence drew me down as if I were falling.

Unfortunately, the only way to descend was by mule or on foot. It took about an hour and a half to traverse the twenty-six switchbacks, sometimes losing sight of the village below.

The Hawaiians lived in relative peace and harmony, free from sickness, for half a millennium, until Captain Cook and other Europeans' arrival. After that, all changed for these island hosts who welcomed foreigners with their spirit of *aloha*.

These asymptomatic strangers stepped on the shore, and a microscopic army began its invasion. As far back as 1823, missionaries started to notice new illnesses coming to the islanders. Over the years, novel diseases such as syphilis, measles, chicken pox, polio, and tuberculosis killed thousands of Hawaiians.

The most hideous of all the plagues was leprosy. It could alter a person's face and hands with lesions and swelling so severe that the islander would be unrecognizable. It struck terror into the hearts of every Hawaiian.

In 1865, King Kamehameha V was so concerned and afraid that this disease would wipe out his subjects; he decided to pass the Act to Prevent Leprosy law.

Sick islanders were rounded up, loaded on a boat bound for Molokai, and deposited in Kalaupapa Bay. The ship didn't even get close to the shore. All had to swim for the beach a half mile away. Many drowned while others were lost in a world of hopelessness.

Eight years later, Father Damien arrived in Kalaupapa. By that time, most of the exiles had died, falling victim to the disease, malnutrition, or exposure. Lawlessness ruled the day.

Father Damien decided to stay with these doomed inhabitants permanently. While attending to his suffering flock, he contracted leprosy and died in the village in 1889.

Jozef De Veuster was born in Tremelo, Belgium, in 1840. He grew up to become an accomplished carpenter. But his life took on the destiny of a priest known as Father Damien.

Called to Molokai, he used his carpentry skills to build houses and churches on the island. He gave all of his exiled fold a newfound hope and purpose to their lives.

As I entered Father Damien's church, I couldn't help but wonder and compare him to another carpenter who tended to lepers, the homeless, and those stricken with disease two thousand years ago.

As I sat in the chapel's pew, I looked down and saw coffee-can-sized holes cut into the floorboards, spaced about every four feet apart. The caretaker explained that leprosy caused the sufferer to lose control of throat muscles where they constantly were drooling with saliva and mucus. So they would take banana leaves and roll them into a funnel, jam it into the hole, and bow their heads without disturbing others as they listened to Father Damien preach.

My hike back up the switchback went faster than I expected. I was lost in thought as I mused in the reflection of Father Damien's incredible story.

The Hawaiians tell their stories in such a beautiful and unique way. Sometimes they sing with their elders' rhythmic chants while other times to the soft swaying of their offspring's hands. Lepers would find a way to tell their stories, realizing that a body can sway, and the words of a story would appear even without the image of a whole human form. These lepers became God's messengers of love as they expressed their gratitude.

As the sun sank into the sea, my mind's eye captured one last rainbow, displaying Molokai's beauty from the deck of our ship. As we sailed back to Maui, I remembered the story told in the seventeenth chapter of the Gospel of Luke.

As Jesus and his disciples were on their way to Jerusalem, they traveled to Samaria and Galilee's border. At a distance, ten lepers called out to Jesus for compassion. Jesus told them to go into the village and show themselves to the priests. And as they went, they became healed.

One of them came back to Jesus, praising God. He threw himself at Jesus's feet and thanked him. Our Lord pointed out to His disciples that only one of the ten lepers returned. And this tenth one was a Samaritan, a foreigner.

Jesus then told the faithful one, "Rise and go, and your faith has made you well."

I can't help but wonder if Father Damien was the eleventh leper!

I returned to the hotel well after nightfall. As I reclined in my Ritz-Carlton poolside lounge chair, listening to Wendy's recount of her happenings of the day, my mind kept drifting back to Kalaupapa, and yet another chant encased with native gratitude!

I would not be cured if the price of the cure was that
I must leave the island and give up my work. I am
perfectly resigned to my lot. Do not feel sorry for me.

—Father Damien

THE RAVEN'S MURMUR

But the Raven sitting lonely on the placid bust, spoke only
That one word, as if his soul in that one word did outpour.
Nothing farther then he uttered—not
a feather then he fluttered—
Till I scarcely more than muttered "Other
friends have flown before—
On the morrow he will leave me, as
my Hopes have flown before."
Then the bird said "Nevermore.

—Edgar Allan Poe, "The Raven"

Ravens are curious creatures. Their intelligence ranks up there with chimpanzees and dolphins. They can even find a way for others to do their bidding.

They can impersonate a fox or wolf call, luring a predator to a carcass. Unable to open the remains itself, the raven waits for the predator to eat, then swoops down to feast on the leftovers, never satisfied with just one bite.

More often than not, ravens are mistaken for a symbol of impending doom, sadness, or depression. I say to the contrary! Did you know that they love to frolic in the snow?

They have been observed walking up a snow-covered bank and then sliding and rolling down it with glee, then walking back up for an encore!

The raven is a social creature. A study in Austria noted that ravens could even point out a target to another bird by using its beak.

And ravens can learn to talk in human language. Yes, they can even bellow out the word, "nevermore."

Whenever I go to Walmart, before I exit my car, I notice a certain raven sitting atop the tallest lamp post. Instead of looking down on the prairie ground life in a distance, this one chooses to gaze on the four-wheeled chariots, scurrying in and out on the hot blacktop with packages askew and carts rolling in all directions.

This bird is a glutton for leftovers as he sits patiently perched, in wait for the discarded trash. It could be soaring over nearby arroyos and lakes, maybe frolicking with others of its kind. No, this one is perfectly content to sit atop its unconventional domain.

The last time I went fishing, a raven descended to investigate one of my lures sitting by the lakeshore. It cocked its head in amazement as it stared at the shiny bauble. After a minute or two of study, it took two hops and flew off.

Here are two different ravens: one who is a loner, content to be away from what other ravens love to do, and the other who sees the attraction, enjoys the moment, and then goes on with its life.

When I was a child in elementary school, my allergies were always a problem. I would show up to class wide awake and sneezing or doped up on meds and sleepy.

Sneezes and runny noses followed by the same repetitive question by student and teacher alike, "Are you sick?"

My answer would always be the same: "No, it's just my allergies. I'm fine."

Little did I know that my weakened immune system would go far beyond weeds and dust and pollen.

I have heard that Hemingway was an avid trout fisherman who loved his taste for strong drink. I loved his masterpiece short story, "The Two-Hearted River." The tale explores the destructive powers of the past versus the serenity of nature in the present.

Did you know that unlike all other fish swimming in the lakes, rivers, and seas, the trout has two hearts? The first heart is a four-chambered heart, just like us humans. It is located just behind the throat and pumps deoxygenated blood to the gills, which allows the fish to take in oxygen and breathe.

The second heart is located near the last vertebrae by the tail. This smaller two-chambered heart doesn't even beat when the fish is in a state of calm. But when the fish is stressed or senses danger and wants to escape, this second heart goes into action.

It starts to beat and pumps blood to the tail and immediately provides the fish with a burst of energy. Not only does the fish fold its fins back with the tail pushing it forward, but its body flaps from side to side to propel it even faster. The fish bolts away by itself until if finally feels that the danger is gone.

Other schooling fish find protection within their school because that's the norm. But when this one who runs away from the school and finally finishes and rests, its second heart ceases to beat and lies in wait for the next time.

I think we alcoholics have two hearts. We go against the norm. When normal people have a drink or two, they enjoy the moment then stop as the sane thing to do. But with an alcoholic, after that first drink, our second heart starts its cadence. Like the trout, we bolt away from the school of normies and continue to run and run until we find ourselves in that darker place.

Like the trout, we bolt away, and we wake up the next day in that insane place. With our second heart silently waiting for the next opportunity.

And whether we are sober for one day or thirty years, we know that the only way to jump-start that second heart is with our next drink.

The Alcoholics Anonymous introductory pamphlet states, "We are perfectly willing to admit that we are allergic to alcohol, and that it is simply common sense to stay away from the source of our allergy."

One could argue, when alcohol enters the body, the alcoholic's weakened immune system has its physical effect accompanied by an overwhelming mental obsession.

Perhaps the allergic reaction is triggered with that burst of energy from the first few drinks and the feeling of euphoria.

Alcoholics refer to alcohol as cunning, baffling, and powerful. And without help, we are doomed. But there is one more powerful than the disease, that one is God!

The sober and recovering in AA start their time together with a moment of silence for the one whose second heart is still in control and ask God to provide serenity for them.

Perhaps what we ask in our serenity prayer is that this second heart will never beat again, and our new sober life will live out its days as God intended for us.

In the last book of the bible, Revelation 21:3–4 NIV, John writes:

> They will be His people, and God Himself will be with them and be their God. He will wipe away every tear from their eyes. There will be no more death or crying or pain, for the old order of things has passed away.

The parking lot is now in shadow as the sun dips behind the Sierra Prieta. My ebony friend atop the lamppost calls out one last time as the shoppers finish their day's spree.

In the distance, others of his kind soar the currents in the waning light above, oblivious to the humans below!

> My life closed twice before its close—
> It yet remains to see
> If immortality unveil
> A third event to me
>
> So huge, so hopeless to conceive,
> As these that twice befell.
> Parting is all we know of heaven,
> And all we need of hell.
>
> —Emily Dickinson, "My Life Closed Twice"

BYDAND

O sad for me Glen Aora,
Where I have friends no more
For lovely lie the rafters,
And the lintels of the door.
The friends are all departed,
The hearth-stone's black and cold,
And sturdy grows the nettle
On the place beloved of old.

There's deer upon the mountain,
There's sheep along the glen,
The forests hum with feather,
But where are now the men?
Here's but my mother's garden
Where soft the footsteps fall,
My folk are quite forgotten,
But the nettle's overall.

—Neil Munro, "Nettles"

I like to go hiking in the Prescott area on the Peavine Trail among the granite dells. Some like it for the lake's panorama, and some admire it for the beauty of the rock formations. I like it because it talks back to me!

After a few hours of walking in solitude, I holler out into the canyon to cut the monotony. My yell is always the same, "Hello!" The boulders' spirit always answers back in the same voice, same sound, and the same person.

About forty-five miles from here, you will find a place called Montezuma Castle. It's not really a castle. It is a canyon where the Sinagua Indians carved out their home in the cliff walls back in the twelfth century.

The only means of egress were a series of makeshift ladders. Their fortress was almost impenetrable to invading enemy tribes.

I wonder if a Sinagua child greeted the dawn of day, high up on the canyon wall, by hollering, "Hello?"

There is a castle in the highlands of Scotland where you might hear the echoes of my ancestry. It is called the Huntly Castle, located by the town of Strathbogie in Aberdeenshire. Right about the same time, the clansmen constructed Huntly Castle, the Sinagua were building their home here in the Arizona desert.

Huntly Castle became the seat of the Clan Gordon shortly after that. Today the ruins of this magnificent palace show the scars of Scottish history. The chief of our clan is the Marquess of Huntly. During the wars for Scottish independence, the Gordons supported William Wallace. Robert the Bruce was said to have stayed in this castle during his travels.

When I was a wee lad of six, I woke up one morning wondering what all the commotion was in our house. My mother and father were scurrying around as they tidied up. They told me today was a special day. It was the day I would meet my uncle Alex.

I couldn't help but notice him when he walked in. After all the hugs, handshakes, and salutations, he looked down at me and said in a thick Scottish brogue, "Sae thes is wee young Lawrence!"

His words were foreign, and my understanding was nil. So I asked him, "Where do you come from?"

His eyes got a little wider as he stared down at me. Then I heard him say, "Ah come frae na Philippines. But I am a highlander just the same!"

Then he bent down, and when we were eyebrow to eyebrow, he peered into my eyes and told me, "An' sae ur ye!"

My mother remembered that our conversation went downhill from there. My side of the discussion was that of asking silly questions: "Where do highlanders sleep at night?" "Do they sleep in the forest?" "Where is your sword?"

That was the first and last time I ever talked to my uncle Alex.

My great-grandfather Alexander Gordon emigrated from Scotland to Connecticut in the late 1840s. My grandfather Lewis Gordon joined the US Navy and found himself fighting under Admiral Dewey in the Philippines during the Spanish–American War. When the war ended, he remained in the islands and built a lucrative sugar plantation business. The land was taken over by Philippine nationalism during the Marcos regime.

Although I have never seen it, I believe in a little town near Aberdeen, Scotland, there is an old cemetery with the gravestone of my great-great-grandfather. Under his name and birth/death date is one word, *bydand*.

The motto of the Gordon Clan is *bydand*. It is a Gaelic word that means "abiding, remaining, and steadfast." Another contraction of *bydand* is a Scots phrase, *bide and fecht*, meaning "to stay and fight."

One of the more famous Gordons to live out his *bydand* was Major General Charles Gordon of Khartoum. He led the

Egyptian held city of Khartoum that was under siege by fifty thousand Mahdist forces.

The Mahdists outnumbered Gordon's defenders seven to one. But Khartoum remained strong for more than ten months, waiting for British reinforcements to arrive.

Two days before the British arrived, the Mahdists over-ran the fortress, killed Gordon and his smaller number of troops, and slaughtered over four thousand civilians.

The Mahdist victory was short-lived. And if you visit Khartoum today, the Mahdists are a forgotten people. The Sudanese will tell you that the most revered man in their ancient city is Pasha Gordon.

Sieges are remembered in human history from Carthage to Leningrad, from Vicksburg to the Alamo. And the one common thread woven in their stand was always *bydand*.

When your spirit is under siege, and all the essential supplies that feed your soul are gone, you stay and fight! Gideon blew his trumpet, David slung his sling, Moses waved his staff, and Rosa Parks claimed her God-given right to sit!

And always, always, at the end of their long struggle was the dawn of a new day for others—that life-giving light of promise on Easter morning.

As the dells cast their long shadows, the sun is setting with Granite Mountain in the foreground. Its diminishing rays still radiate splashes of golden beams as it retreats below the mountain's profile.

For tomorrow, this east-facing rock will shine with the Lord's first light yet again as it was in the beginning.

On the sixth day of creation, God completed his work and saw all that he had made, and it was good. Then as dawn's early rays kissed the earth, he rested and blessed the new day and made it holy.

It was the seventh sunrise!

As I live out my senior years in the highlands of Arizona, the words of Uncle Alex and Sister Fran still echo in my mind. My life is measured by sunrises and sunsets.

Before it was day
I climbed to meet the sun
half way
on the side of a mountain.
A high cool pond
poured down over rocks
to a slow dreamy valley
singing of new born clouds.
Facing the warm reflections
on the quiet sky
I bowed and kissed the dew
on the young grass.
But soon I felt guilty
What had I done?
What is the dew
on young grass?

—William Saphier, "Before Sunrise"

GRATITUDES

I want to thank my entire extended family for their continuing support and love while writing my book during this global pandemic especially my daughter, Heidi; son, Tim; sister, Janet; my goddaughter, Denise; my grandchildren, Tim, Scott, Steven, Samantha, Zack, Madison, Hailey, Lynah, Hannah, Ricky, and Wendy; and my great-grandchildren, Zander, Malayah, Jaxton, Lance, Ryker, Kinsley, and Lacy.

And to those who have passed on, my beloved wife, Wendy; my son, Scott; my mother, Persis, and father, Robert; Sister Fran; cousin, Carol; uncles, Bob, Alex, Louie, and Frank; and aunts Pat, Mildred, and Jenny. I am thankful for Wendy's grandmother, Helen Groote and the entire Anderson family for the memory of Velma Anderson. They all provided me with the inspiration to tell these stories.

I am grateful to Adam Bissell and those who helped establish the Heart Song Center for Grieving Children in Prescott, Arizona, and the staff of the New Song Center for Grieving Children in Phoenix, Arizona.

The source of the activity "Keys to Our Feelings" is from "The Dougy Center for Grieving Children," *Waving Goodbye Activities Manual*, 2004, p. 32. The Message Version (MSG) of Genesis 1 in the Bible was used to introduce each chapter of the book.

My appreciation goes to the Parknowitz, Short, and Kirchmer families for the beautiful memory of their mother and grandmother, Mary Short, and to the Hale family for their loved one, Marie Hughes.

My gratitude goes to the Paternostro family for the memories created with Elaine and Dominic.

I thank my friend, Hank. There is no greater blessing than to have a friendship that lasts over seven decades.

Thank you to my friend, Patty, for her friendship and meaningful conversations.

I am also grateful to my former confirmation and Sunday school students, all eight hundred of them. They provided me with many years of wonderful lessons of life and spirit.

Finally, I want to thank the staff at Christian Faith Publishers who brought my manuscript to life especially my literary agent, Linda Hewlett, and publication specialist, Melissa Wagner, for their personal care and follow-through.

ACKNOWLEDGMENTS

Aeschylus (Greek author and playwright, 525/524 BC–456/455 BC). "Even in my sleep, pain which cannot forget falls drop by drop upon my heart until in my own despair, against my will, comes wisdom through the awful grace of God."

Aurelius, Marcus (Roman emperor, AD 121–AD 180). "Nowhere can a man find a quieter or more untroubled retreat than his own soul."

Barrie, J. M. (Scottish novelist, 1860–1937). 1904. *Peter Pan*. "Fairies have to be one thing or the other because being so small they unfortunately have room for only one feeling at a time."

Beecher, Henry Ward (American minister, 1813–1887). "Children are the hands by which we take hold of heaven."

Blake, William (English poet, 1757–1827). 1794. "The Tyger."

Bonhoeffer, Dietrich (German theologian, 1906–1945). "We must learn to regard people less in the light of what they do or omit to do and more in the light of what they suffer."

Bunyan, John (English writer, 1628–1688). 1678. *Pilgrim's Progress*. "It is always hard to see the purpose in wilderness wanderings until they are over."

Colton, Charles Caleb (English cleric and writer, 1780–1832). "Peace is the evening star in the sky, as virtue is its sun, and the two are never far apart."

Confucius (Chinese philosopher, 551 BC–479 BC). "It does not matter how slowly you go as long as you do not stop."

de Saint-Exupery, Antoine (French writer, 1900–1944). 1943. *The Little Prince.*

Descartes, Rene (French philosopher, 1596–1650). "We do not describe the world we see, we see the world we can describe."

Dickinson, Emily (American poet, 1830–1886). 1896. "My Life Closed Twice."

Donne, John (English poet, 1572–1631). 1624. "For Whom the Bell Tolls."

Dostoevsky, Fyodor (Russian novelist, 1821–1881). "Every any knows the formula of its ant-hill. Every bee know the formula of its beehive. They know it in their own way, not in our way. Only humankind does not know its own formula."

Ellis, Havelock (physician, 1859–1939). "The Promised Land always lies on the other side of a wilderness."

Emerson, Ralph Waldo (American essayist, 1803–1882). "What lies behind us and what lies ahead of us are tiny matters to what lies within us."

"Nature always wears the colors of the spirit."

Father Damien (Roman Catholic priest, 1840–1889). "I would not be cured if the price of the cure was that I must leave the island and give up my work. I am perfectly resigned to my lot. Do not feel sorry for me."

Franklin, Benjamin (Founding Father of the United States, 1706–1790). "Life can only be understood backwards, but it must be lived forwards."

"All mankind is divided into three classes: those that are immovable, those that are movable, and those that move."

Frost, Robert (American poet, 1874–1963). 1916. "The Road Not Taken." "In three words I can sum up everything I've learned about life: It goes on."

Fuller, Thomas (English churchman and historian, 1608–1661). "Music is nothing else but wild sounds civilized into time and tune."

Gandhi, Mahatma (Indian lawyer, 1869–1948). "Joy lies in the fight, in the attempt, in the suffering involved, not in the victory itself."

Hearn, Lafcaido (Greek-Japanese writer, 1850–1904). "All good work is done the way ants do things; little by little!"

Henley, William Ernest (British poet and writer, 1849–1903). 1875. "Invictus."

James, Henry (American-British author, 1843–1916). "Three things in human life are important. The first is to be kind; the second is to be kind, the third is to be kind."

Keller, Helen (American writer, 1880–1968). "The best and most beautiful things in this world, cannot be seen or even touched—they must be felt with the heart."

Kierkegaard, Soren (Danish philosopher, 1813–1855). "Life can only be understood backwards, but it must be lived forwards."

Lowell, James Russell (American poet, 1819–1891). 1904. "She Came and Went."

MacDonagh, Michael (British journalist, 1860–1946). 1916. "The Irish at the Front."

Mann, Horace (American educator, 1796–1859). "Be ashamed to die until you have won some victory for humanity."

Melville, Herman (American novelist, 1819–1891). 1851. *Moby Dick.* "It is not down on any map, true places never are."

Milton, John (English poet, 1608–1674). 1645. "L'Allegro." "The stars that nature hung in heaven, and filled their lamps with everlasting oil, give due light to the misled and lonely traveler."

Munro, Neil (Scottish journalist, 1863–1930). 1917. "Nettles

O'Neill, Eugene (American playwright, 1888–1953). "Life is a solitary cell where walls are mirrors!"

Saint Francis of Assisi (Catholic priest, died 1226) 1912. Prayer of Saint Francis.

Sandburg, Carl (American poet, 1876–1967). 1918. "Wilderness," Cornhuskers original collection.

Saphier, William (Romanian/American poet, 1886–1942) 1920. "Conscience" and "Before Sunrise."

Seattle, Chief (Suquamish/Duwamish chief, died 1866). "Humankind has not woven the web of life. We are but one thread within it. Whatever we do to the web, we do it to ourselves. All things are bound together. All things connect."

Shakespeare, William (English playwright, 1564–1616). "New friends may be poems but old friends are alphabets. Don't forget the alphabets because you will need them to read the poems."

Southey, Robert (English poet, 1774–1843) early nineteenth century. "What Are Little Boys Made Of?"

Spurgeon, Charles H. (preacher, 1834–1892). "Hope itself is like a star—not to be seen in the sunshine of prosperity and only to be discovered in the night of adversity."

Thoreau, Henry David (American naturalist, 1817–1862). 1854. *Walden.* "Many men go fishing all of their lives without knowing that it is not the fish they are after."

"Heaven is under our feet as well as over our heads."

Twain, Mark (American writer, 1835–1910). "When I was a boy of seventeen, my father was so ignorant. I could hardly stand to have the old man around. But when I got to be twenty-one, I was astonished at how much he had learned in seven years!"

"Whenever you find yourself on the side of the majority, it is time to pause and reflect."

Wilde, Oscar (Irish poet, 1854–1900). "With freedom, books, flowers, and the moon, who could not be happy?"

Wordsworth, William (English poet, 1770–1850). 1798. *Lyrical Ballads,.* "Odes on Imitations of Immortality from Recollections of Early Childhood," 1804.

Yeats, William Butler (Irish poet, 1865–1839). 1934. "Conjunctions."

ABOUT THE AUTHOR

Larry Gordon was born in Hollywood, California. As a child, he was always intrigued by dawn's early light. He remembers watching the sun's first rays come up over the Mulholland Hills on Easter morning to the herald of trumpets and angelic choir voices in the Hollywood Bowl.

His curiosity about how magnificent the sunrise must have been on the day God rested led to his book, *The Seventh Sunrise*.

After a successful business career in the relocation industry, he lives his days in the highlands of Arizona. His hobbies include hiking, fly-fishing, reading, and writing.

He is a grateful father of three, grandfather of eleven, and great-grandfather of seven.

His faith has led him in several endeavors: Sunday school and confirmation teacher, facilitator in a center for grieving children, active member in Survivors of Suicide, a big brother, and volunteer hospital chaplain.

CPSIA information can be obtained
at www.ICGtesting.com
Printed in the USA
BVHW011947110423
662161BV00014B/146

9 781638 445531